BRILLIANT MISTAKES

Finding Success on the Far Side of Failure

Paul J. H. Schoemaker

Wharton
DIGITAL PRESS

Philadelphia

Published by Wharton Digital Press
The Wharton School
University of Pennsylvania
3620 Locust Walk
2000 Steinberg Hall-Dietrich Hall
Philadelphia, PA 19104

Ebook ISBN: 978-1-61363-011-2
Paperback ISBN: 978-1-61363-012-9

Dedication in Memoriam

This book is dedicated to the memory of Robert E. Gunther. Over the course of several decades, Robert and I collaborated on three earlier books and various articles. He also provided invaluable editorial support on countless other projects. Along the way, he became a dear friend. In 2006, we coauthored an article for the *Harvard Business Review* titled "The Wisdom of Deliberate Mistakes." That article provided the impetus for this book.

Robert and I worked as coauthors for over a year to conceptualize *Brilliant Mistakes* as a book. We hoped to produce a popular trade book that would reach a general audience. With the generous and expert help of our literary agent, Jill Marsal, we collaborated on a proposal and outlines for each chapter. Sadly, Robert died in the summer of 2009 before our proposal was ready. Simultaneously, the market for trade books experienced a decline, which further delayed completion.

I hope that Robert would have approved of *Brilliant Mistakes* in its new form. As I reworked the manuscript, I missed Robert's keen mind, turn of phrase, deep curiosity, and remarkable work ethic. More than all else, I especially miss his friendship. As difficult as it was to deal with his loss and move forward, I am grateful I had the chance to work with Robert and to witness the strength, grace, and courage he brought to his fight with a very tough illness. I am happy that the project we began together has finally come to fruition, for his family's benefit and in his memory.

Contents

Preface

Mistakes...are the portals of discovery.
—JAMES JOYCE[1]

If you have ever flown in an airplane, taken an antibiotic, or used electricity from a nuclear power plant, you have first-hand experience with the power of mistakes. Each one of those innovations resulted from a flash or two of brilliant insight and many, many years of wrong answers, dead ends, and missteps.[2]

The ill-fated flight at Kitty Hawk showed how an idea that seems impossibly wrong can be achieved by two Wrights. Alexander Fleming's accidental discovery of penicillin, the world's first and most successful antibiotic, involved a sloppy lab, keen perception, and an exceptionally well-prepared mind. Scientists labored for decades to harness nuclear power, beginning with Einstein's landmark 1905 article in the *Annals of Physics* arguing that mass (m) can be converted into energy (E) via the formula $E = mc^2$ (where c is the speed of light).[3] Even though Einstein's articles were brilliantly original, they contained numerous mistakes, at least 23 according to one careful study (see appendix A). However, many of these errors were actually helpful, and some even necessary, to sustain Einstein in developing his revolutionary theories about mass, energy, gravity, time, and space.[4]

It would take several more decades before another brilliant scientist, Enrico Fermi, provided irrefutable empirical evidence in support of Einstein's famous formula. Using a converted squash court at the University of Chicago, Fermi was able to achieve the first-ever controlled release of nuclear energy in 1942. He later joined Oppenheimer's Manhattan Project in Los Alamos, where they developed the world's first atomic bomb, building on the earlier experiments in that converted squash court. The atom bomb shows Einstein's formula that $E = mc^2$ with a big bang and brought the Second World War to a quick end. It also shows that mistakes can be beneficial to discovery and may be necessary to arrive at deep new insights. Even a genius like Einstein could not do without them.

Brilliant Mistakes examines the beneficial side of error by considering mistakes as "portals of discovery." Through stories and analysis, I show that it's possible to design for brilliant mistakes—those that accelerate learning and lead to breakthrough innovation—and to avoid tragic ones. I also argue that all mistakes are not created equal. Some have high cost and offer little learning value, while others cost little and produce deep, valuable insight. These are the brilliant mistakes, the ones to embrace rather than avoid. This book will teach you how to recognize, foster, and reward them in yourself and others.

Think about the last time you tried something new, whether it was acquiring a language, learning a new sport, or starting a company. Did you make errors along the way? Did those errors help or hinder your progress toward your goal? The path from insight to discovery is seldom a straight line. Most groundbreaking achievements in science, technology, economics, and the arts represent long, meandering paths of misjudgments and false turns. Indeed, our very existence as humans relies on the error mechanism of random mutation; we would not exist if our evolutionary process had not included a few hiccups and false turns. But it isn't enough just to accept that mistakes are part of progress. We can do better than simply rely on random error to eventually point the way. We can, and should, learn to be strategic about the errors we allow.

Unfortunately, the systems that surround us make this a difficult proposition. Our schools and organizations are designed for efficiency and order. These are fine principles but rarely encourage mistakes, either brilliant or foolish. Students are graded on how much they know, not on the degree to which they learn from helpful errors. Similarly, companies strive for error elimination, hiring advisers and relying on sophisticated management tools such as Six Sigma.[5] It's little wonder, then, that most decision-making books follow suit, encouraging you to focus narrowly on mistake avoidance today rather than provoking you to plan for the stream of decisions that you will face tomorrow.

Ironically, the University of Chicago, that bulwark of rational economic thinking propelled by Milton Friedman and other Nobel laureates in economics, launched the first academic center among business schools to study our less rational side. As a faculty member at the business school's Center for Decision Research, I spent twelve years among colleagues doing research on subjects that seemed, to some at the time, esoteric and off-kilter. We studied how experienced executives could be blinded by their frames of mind or why numerous traps and biases might cloud their judgment and choices. At first, most esteemed economists looked askance at our studies and findings.[6] Paradoxically, it turned out to be a brilliant mistake for the University of Chicago's business school to encourage a small group of intellectually diverse scholars to challenge basic tenets underlying the rational economic model.

The field of behavioral decision theory has since gained great momentum across multiple academic disciplines. The principles that underlie it—such as the idea that humans are error-prone, that consumers exhibit predictable biases, and that markets are not always efficient—have gained wide attention and infiltrated popular thought. In 2002, the Nobel Prize in Economics was awarded to Daniel Kahneman, a psychologist who was then at Princeton University. Such lofty recognition for research done by someone outside of economics is quite unusual, although not unprecedented.[7] Kahneman's groundbreaking work in prospect theory as well as heuristics and biases, research he conducted mostly with another brilliant cognitive psychologist, the late Amos Tversky, showed that people's decisions are strongly influenced by psychological factors.

The mantle of behavioral decision theory has been worn by many others and has spawned an active research community. The Society for Judgment and Decision Making counts over 1,000 academic members, many of who conduct research.[8] Popular books drawing on the field, with such titles as *Freakonomics, Predictably Irrational*, and *Nudge*, fill book shelves and e-readers.[9] This new behavioral discipline is also embraced by government leaders, including advisers in the Obama administration who wish to explore new approaches to health care, education, and other thorny policy issues.[10]

In this book, I build on the strong theoretical foundation of decades of research in decision psychology as well as behavioral economics and go even a step further. I offer a practical plan for separating destructive from constructive mistakes and for learning to make more of the brilliant kind. By exploring how to access mistakes for their learning potential, I will encourage you to challenge cherished assumptions and improve your future prospects. I will even, at times, suggest that you make mistakes on purpose—all in the spirit of challenging false beliefs and accelerating learning. I will not simply encourage you to accept that you, like every other person on the planet, are error-prone—I will encourage you to embrace this quality, to milk it for all of its evolutionary and learning potential.

The stories, frameworks, and insights of this book emphasize the following key messages:

1. It is important to embrace the learning potential of mistakes—first, by overcoming the shame and fear that lead us to overlook the covert messages they carry about how we think.
2. To learn from a mistake, it's critical to separate the decision process—the part that you own—from the outcomes, which are usually influenced by external factors.
3. There is a difference between silly errors and brilliant mistakes, and it all hinges on the relative costs and benefits of what is at stake. Designing for, and learning from, a mistake can make it brilliant.
4. In some cases, it's advisable to allow room for mistakes to be made. Just as random mutations have advanced evolution, clever, well-designed mistakes can further human progress by opening new vistas.

For most people, the problem is not that they make too many mistakes but too few. Ask a few elderly people you know about their areas of greatest regret, and most will recount errors of omission rather than commission—what they failed to do rather than what they did. People are quick to agree that in retrospect, one can learn much from mistakes, and that some mistakes therefore can have great value. When I ask experienced managers in executive programs what they have learned from most in life, they usually say mistakes. When I reply, "Since mistakes have been so valuable to you, why don't you make a few more?" they tend to look back at me with puzzled faces. The idea of purposeful mistakes runs counter to the zero-tolerance management approach of reducing error whenever and wherever possible.

Brilliant Mistakes provides a road map for designing for and learning from error. It helps you assess your own decision-making process and clear through the brush of the emotional and cognitive reactions, like shame or the deflection of blame, that tend to cloud your ability to learn from your own mistakes. I provide insights about how and why you make decisions, and I offer processes to improve your judgment and choices. I also go further and explore a controversial question: if a few mistakes can be good, wouldn't a few more be even better? To learn maximally from mistakes, we need to commit more errors than we deem optimal as judged within the bounds of our limited rationality. This idea may be hard to swallow. Yet it is the quintessential insight of this book, made practical through example, exposition, and advice on when and how to make smart mistakes.

It's my hope that this book will help you be a little less perfect—and a little wiser about and tolerant of mistakes. If you follow its guiding principles, you will gain new insight about different types of errors we make, and you'll learn how to recognize situations in which mistakes could be beneficial. Along the way, you'll come to accept the counterintuitive notion that we sometimes should deliberately commit errors, as they may be our only chance to move to greater under-standing. I look forward to guiding you to your own portals of discovery, knowing that these portals will help you in business and beyond.

Introduction
When Wrong Is Right

On a frigid New Year's morning, an obscure music group auditioned for an executive at one of the world's leading record companies. After years of modest success playing local clubs, this band was looking for their big break. In order to make it to this audition, they had braved a ten-hour ride through a blinding snowstorm. Their driver had gotten lost, but they had still arrived before the executive, who had been toasting in the New Year the night before. This band was one of many he would audition that year, including at least one other audition later that same day. Band and executive were both exhausted. The band's equipment was dilapidated from months on the road; the studio executive substituted his own amplifiers. It was not an auspicious beginning.

Once in the studio, the band spent an hour taping a dozen songs. This tape ended up in the hands of the seasoned head of the artist and repertoire (A&R) department for Vox Music, a prominent label. He turned it down. The style of the band's music, he felt, was on the way out. He was in good company. A few weeks earlier, the general marketing manager of Epsilon Records, another top recording company, had also checked out this same band and come to the same conclusion. In a letter to the group, Epsilon's general marketing manager made the following curt assessment: "While we

appreciate the talents of this group, we feel that we have sufficient groups of this type at the present time under contract.
It would not be advisable for us to sign any further contracts
of this nature." Around the same time, two other recording
companies listened to the band, and the reply was the same:
a polite or impolite but emphatic no. In total, the band was
turned down by at least four respected recording companies
after getting a fair hearing at each.

"With Every Mistake We Must Surely Be Learning"

That should have been the end of the story. One card,
however, remained in play. The head of A&R for one of
Epsilon's smallest labels was out of town during the general
manager's deliberations. His absence seemed a small matter
at the time, since this label was—according to one Epsilon
insider—the "joker in the pack, and not just because it
released many comedy records. In terms of budget, hits, and
prestige it was the poor relation of the company's powerful
labels." With the exception of a label devoted to Salvation Army
Bands, it was Epsilon's poorest performer. What could this
manager possibly add to the evaluation of an up-and-coming
rock band? More respected executives, closer to this genre of
music, had already rendered a verdict of thumbs-down.

But six months later, the band's persistent manager
brought its audition tapes through the back door of Epsilon
and appealed to the head of this small label. This young
maverick was both passionate and ambitious. After a stint in
the navy, he had joined Epsilon as an assistant to the manager.
He sought out new and untapped bands and developed niche
markets, such as comedy records, into profitable businesses.
Five years later, at age 29, he would assume leadership of the
label, making him the youngest label chief in Epsilon's history.
He had a prescient understanding of how new recording technologies would have an impact on the future of the music

industry. Because he was forced to feed on the scraps of the corporation's artists, he developed close working relationships with talent, in contrast to the typical arm's-length relationships of most managers. He was eager to change the world.

This manager was intrigued by what he heard on the band's demo. He decided to invite them back for another audition. During the audition, he was more impressed by their wit and potential than by the music they played for him, but he decided to sign them nonetheless. All this happened just six months after the best minds of the very same recording company had turned the band down. There had always been independent decision making at Epsilon labels, but this reversal came as a bit of a surprise to Epsilon's general manager, who was responsible for multiple labels. After the contract was inked, he wrote to the band with a hint of embarrassment to explain "what may appear to you to be an anomaly in our Organization. I can assure you that the artist managers did hear the record but I know you will appreciate that even artist managers are human and can change their minds!" How could a comedy album executive be signing a rock band, against the better judgment of senior colleagues who truly had their fingers on the pulse of the industry? This was surely a mistake, right?

What's Your View?
- Was the comedy album manager wise to sign the band through the back door?
- Should Epsilon's general manager have blocked signing the band a second time?
- Was the band at fault for showing up late for the audition, without all equipment?
- Was the band smart in reapproaching Epsilon Records through the back door?

Most people read this case and decide that it was a mistake for the label to sign the band—that is, unless they are fans of music history and recognize the details of the story or pick up the clue in the title to this section. Here's a hint: it's a quote from their famous song "While My Guitar Gently Weeps."

You've got it: this story is about the discovery of the Beatles. The young executive was George Martin of the Parlophone label at EMI (disguised as Epsilon Records). By ignoring conventional wisdom and making a move most would deem a "mistake," Martin helped his company become a dominant player in the recording business. As Beatlemania spread across the globe, the Fab Four became one of the most successful groups of all time, selling over a billion records internationally. They sold more albums in the United States and earned more number one albums on UK charts than any other band. Decca, the recording company that passed on the Beatles after the January 1962 studio audition (disguised, in this anecdote, as Vox), is now famous for what seems the most glaring oversight in music history. Especially ironic, in hindsight, is their declaration at the time that "groups of guitars are on the way out."[11] Instead, they signed Brian Poole & the Tremeloes. How many people still remember *that* group?

The Path to Brilliance

I've opened this book with the Beatles' discovery story because it illustrates one of the central propositions of this book: the degree to which assumptions deeply held by the best and brightest can be wrong and the enormous potential benefit of seeing past them and making a brilliant mistake. Assumptions can be wrong for numerous reasons, ranging from changes in the world in which the assumptions were formed to lack of humility among those at the top. In the case of all of the Vox executives, and all but one of the Epsilon executives, many of these factors were probably in place.

That leaves us with George Martin. What did *he* know that nobody else knew? In truth, we know too little about Martin's inner thought process to be sure. He could have simply been foolish and lucky. As we'll see throughout this book, many stories of great discoveries can be interpreted as entirely reliant on dumb luck. It's also possible that he saw that the world was changing and that the assumptions his industry was built on would not continue to hold in the future.[12] To the extent that the latter is true, he's a great example of someone who was able to understand himself and the world around him well enough to make the risky, high-reward move of a brilliant mistake.

George Martin certainly wouldn't have viewed his signing the Beatles as a mistake. No self-respecting manager would ever knowingly make a mistake. Like Martin, managers view their role as taking calculated risks that yield, on average, a positive payoff. But if the Beatles had indeed been a huge flop, as many in the industry expected, we would now consider Martin's decision a mistake. Luckily for him, the opposite happened. The Beatles rose to global dominance in pop music. In retrospect, Martin is viewed as a visionary who made a brilliant decision. But should our judgment about whether Martin's decision was brilliant or misguided really hinge so much on that remarkable outcome? If someone wins the lottery, was buying that winning ticket a good decision on that occasion (and a bad one most other times when the payoff was nil)? Few of us would scold a friend who won the lottery for having been so wasteful. Instead, we congratulate the person, with perhaps a touch of envy. But shouldn't we, in all fairness, base our assessment on what our friend or someone like George Martin could reasonably have known and predicted prior to the decision? Many theorists would argue that this should be the standard of judgment, without the distortions due to knowledge obtained in hindsight.

Once we adopt this theoretically pure standard, another issue arises. Can we ever judge fairly, in hindsight, whether a decision was smart or dumb? To what extent can we put ourselves in the shoes of someone else and ignore all other information, including what happened after the decision? Before you learned that the band was the Beatles, who did *you* side with: the seasoned executives or the young manager? The challenge in understanding mistakes is that we make decisions looking forward and judge them in hindsight. How do you determine what is a good mistake in light of this? And what is the difference between taking a risk and making a mistake? George Martin intuitively appreciated the difference between a dumb mistake and a brilliant one. In signing the Beatles, Martin minimized his downside risks. As he commented later, "To say I was taking a gamble would be stretching it, because the deal I offered them was pretty awful." The Beatles received one penny for each record sold. At the time Martin made his offer, the Beatles were happy to take any contract with a major label such as EMI.[13] Although he wrote a tightwad contract, Martin could have signed another band that would have had a higher likelihood of success, so he took a risk nonetheless.

This book examines why a set of popular views of mistakes may be deeply mistaken and offers a new way of looking at (and benefiting from) mistakes. I begin with the view that there are four different kinds of mistakes (tragic, serious, trivial, and brilliant), and then I turn to the practical question of how we can err our way to success. The main benefit of mistakes is that they speed learning. Martin's decision changed the music industry. Even though there was already a trend in the making, it might not have flourished quite the way it did if gatekeepers had continued to sign the same acts. Repeating the same formula over and over builds expertise in a narrow field—a form of accretive learning. As physicist Niels Bohr (1885–1962) said, "An expert is a person who has made all the mistakes that are possible in a very narrow field."[14] Brilliant mistakes, in contrast, expand the field and accelerate learning beyond the narrow confines of conventional wisdom. This is expansive rather than convergent learning. Sometimes there is no way to reach a destination through incremental accumulation of knowledge, just as you cannot cross a chasm in small steps. You need to take the leap of brilliant mistakes. Mistakes can speed learning in areas from advertising to hiring people to speed dating, as we shall discuss, and you can design mistakes for maximum benefit.

Beyond individual mistakes, it's also possible to foster ecosystems at an organizational or even a societal level that allow mistakes to have broad benefit. How can we optimize our portfolios of mistakes? How can we make fewer tragic and serious mistakes and not be distracted by trivial ones? How can we recognize and encourage brilliant mistakes? EMI's Ron White, who had turned down the Beatles personally, created an organization that allowed Martin to sign the band through the back door. This kind of slack, which is largely absent in many companies today, fosters opportunities for creativity and innovation. White appreciated this diversity and the willingness of managers to change their minds about past decisions, even if it meant writing a letter of apology to the Beatles to clarify what might appear to be an "anomaly" in their organization. Diverse thinking and tolerance for mistakes are both critical to innovation since they allow for variation beyond what is normally seen. At times, we need to design ecosystems of mistakes.

Real-life mistakes are complex and messy. Although many autobiographies paint an incomplete and self-serving picture of what led the author to greatness, many successful people have honestly acknowledged the role of mistakes in their own lives. The concluding chapter recounts how leaders in diverse fields have leveraged mistakes to advantage. From Albert Einstein to Jack Welch, we shall see that mistakes played a crucial role in the success of many remarkable people. Using their stories and other famous successes, we shall offer a practical and very personal view of the principles discussed throughout the book. The key message is that mistakes are essential to success and that most people don't look at mistakes in the right way. Few of us use mistakes as fully as we can. As Eleanor Roosevelt said, "Learn from the mistakes of others. You can't live long enough to make them all yourself."

The first part of the book, "Rethinking Mistakes," examines the meaning of mistakes and their often hidden value. It argues that we need to change our thinking about mistakes in rather fundamental ways to reap their full benefits. The second part, "Designing for Mistakes," examines strategies for making mistakes on purpose to increase the odds of brilliance. Creative industries, from movie production to basic science, are better at tolerating mavericks. Sometimes crazy ideas and unlikely performers become phenomenal successes, as demonstrated by programs such as *American Idol* (or the surprising discovery of Susan Boyle in the British version) that cast a very wide net to turn up some unlikely successes. Even so, as shown by the initial refusal to sign the Beatles, established players often suffer from blind spots and hubris that prevent them from seeing new opportunities. Many industries and professions don't appreciate the full power of mistakes. Unwittingly, they pursue narrow strategies shrouded in tunnel vision.

This book isn't about luck, or coincidences, or gut feel. It's about deliberate, process-driven, intelligent mistakes: presumed errors that challenge the status quo and lead to immeasurably advantageous outcomes. But before we get there—before we play out a strategy for making smart mistakes—we need to establish what mistakes are and why they happen.

Part One
Rethinking Mistakes

CHAPTER 1

Context Matters
Defining Mistakes

Life can only be understood backwards;
but it must be lived forwards.
—SØREN KIERKEGAARD[15]

George Martin's signing of the Beatles was a calculated risk that likely seemed foolish at the time to everyone except him. Along the way, music paradigms shifted, beliefs were overturned, and pop music was rewritten. History is replete with similar tales of iconoclasts, some of whom risked it all, like the Wright brothers, who gave up their successful bicycle business to follow their dream of flight. Cyrus McCormick also was a single-minded inventor: his house and his farm were both repossessed while he pursued his vision of a mechanical reaper to harvest. He launched a tractor company, International Harvester, which became one of the most successful American businesses of the early 20th century. Martin, the Wright brothers, and McCormick certainly must have seemed, at the time, like foolish dreamers, but the vicissitudes of history have mostly polished their stories to a gleam. Decisions that once seemed foolhardy now look brilliant.

Retrospect, of course, lends the past a false clarity. The hindsight bias, a well-known and much-studied illusion in human judgment,[16] clouds any attempt to glean useful insights from these or any other stories. In this chapter, I present a set of criteria to help you recognize brilliant mistakes in the here and now, so you don't have to wait for history to sort the wheat from the chaff. I encourage you to learn faster by running experiments with benefits that you *can't* be certain of or defend easily ahead of time. I will show you how to recognize, and deliberately make, clever mistakes.

Theory

Let's begin with a comprehensive definition of a mistake. Merriam-Webster defines a mistake as "a wrong action or statement proceeding from faulty judgment, inadequate knowledge, or inattention."[17] This crisp definition relies on a simple outcomes-based criterion of truth. It lacks nuance and fails to account for near-misses or for good-enough answers. If we accept this definition, we then must consider any prediction or action that fails to achieve its intended goal—from the soccer ball that glances past the goal, to the economist's prediction of growth in GNP at 3.1% when the actual growth was 3.09%—to be an error.

A strict outcomes-based definition falls short in other regards as well. First, it fails to account for either the complexity of the world we live in or the existence of simple bad luck. In reality, we spend most of our lives operating from incomplete knowledge and limited understanding. As such, most of our judgments and actions could be deemed mistakes by that count alone. In addition, outcomes of our predictions, actions, or decisions are usually subject to random chance. Would we call a surgeon who loses a patient to a freak complication—one that could not have been fore-seen based on the best available evidence—"mistake-prone"? According to the Merriam-Webster's definition, the patient's death alone is the sole determinant of whether the doctor acted correctly or incorrectly.

Both religion and classical decision theory provide alter-native models. In religion, outcomes are not the ultimate standard of the quality of an individual's decision. Instead, what matters is whether the decision maker abides by key principles or moral laws. Similarly, decision theory, an academic field devoted to the study of rational choice, focuses on the thought process that *precedes* a decision rather than the outcomes that follow it. Let's say that you were trying to decide whether or not to quit your job and pursue an acting career: would this be a mistake? According to decision theorists, the answer would lie not in whether you eventually landed on the silver screen but in whether you had evaluated your strengths, considered other options, assessed their benefits and risks, and selected according to your deepest preferences. In this view, the only mistake you can make is a failure to follow an informed and well-reasoned decision process. A decision theorist would probably chide you for playing games like roulette in a casino or the state lottery with slim hopes of winning (unless you argue that you were doing so *merely* for the sake of entertainment). This theorist would point out that the odds were stacked against you, and would try to argue that your dollars would be better invested in the stock market since it has historically yielded a positive payoff.

For this book, I define a mistake as *a decision, an action, or a judgment that is less than optimal, given what was possible to know at the time.* In other words, I emphasize the *input* side of mistakes rather than the end result. This definition will be familiar to scholars of decision science but less so to leaders in the business world. In a competitive world, driven by quarterly targets and high shareholder expectations, it's hard to argue for the inherent value of a good decision process. Companies typically reward results, not just good plans or thoughtful deliberation. But it's my belief—and this book will build the case—that process-driven decisions will, in the long run, yield better results than those that are primarily rewarded by outcomes.

Reality

Let's leave the rarefied world of theory and consider how our definition of *mistake* holds up to light and air. Consider a salesperson in any industry. To figure out whether or not this salesperson is making mistakes, it would be simplest to just look at their revenue targets, and at whether or not they were meeting them. Right? That would be an outcomes-based way of determining the mistake-proneness of that salesperson.

Now try the same thought experiment with the process criterion. We would have to examine *how* various sales judgments were made. How did the salesperson allocate his time? What assumptions did he make about key accounts? What angle of his product did he play up in critical meetings or fail to mention? Once we collect all of these data, we *then* have to judge whether, along this spectrum of small decisions, the salesperson was making mistakes. Furthermore, we would need to assess whether or not he had sufficient information that could or should have helped him avoid errors. Clearly, this isn't an easy proposition. Right about now, you might be thinking: that outcomes-based definition of *mistake* might not be so bad, after all. Isn't it so much simpler and far more objective to look at results, not process? Outcomes-based definitions of mistakes are just, well, easier to determine.

Sure, it's simpler and more objective (although seemingly objective numbers can be fudged as well at times). But also, this outcomes-based method is more likely to lead you to erroneous conclusions about a person's performance. Various factors—beside the decision itself—can influence a decision's outcomes, as illustrated in figure 1-1.

Each of these factors has the potential to blind us about the quality of a decision, to lead us away from the path of truly understanding another person's judgment toward quick but potentially false and unfair conclusions. To separate out each of these factors, think of them as elements

Fig 1-1 Factors Impacting a Decision's Outcomes

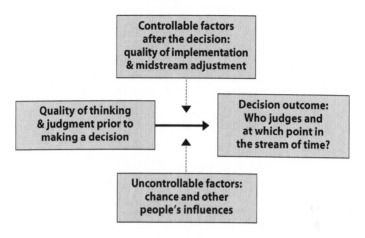

that might confuse, distort, or distract us from seeing the full picture:

1. **Temporality.** We may not be able to see *all* consequences of a decision at the time we judge its quality, as some long-term consequences may be still playing out. At what point in the continuum from initiation of a decision to its final consequence do we stop and say, Here, this is the moment when we can see its impact? Many important decisions, from divorce to starting a company, have a very long tail.

2. **Chance.** Random events may have significantly influenced the outcome in the decision we are evaluating. Think how illness might affect a student's grades, how bad weather can ruin a picnic or affect school test results or voter turnout. By definition, randomness cannot be predicted. In most decisions of consequence, where the stakes are high and the issues complex, chance usually plays a significant role.

3. **Treatment effects.** These are actions taken after the decision, by either the decision maker or others, that may further change its course. When President Jimmy Carter proclaimed on television that the country was suffering from a malaise, not only did he make a prediction about the true state of affairs, he also created a self-fulfilling prophecy. Suppose your company has a fast-track program for high-potential managers. Suppose further that these selected few indeed do far better in their careers: is it due to the company's ability to scout and select for talent or their ability to train them well (that is, the treatment they got after having been selected)?

4. **Missing data.** How would alternatives that were omitted when the decision was made have played out? If we fail to consider what the other choices available at the time would have yielded, can we ever really know if we made the best decision? Suppose that new salesperson you hired worked out really well. You would be pleased and conclude, naturally, that you had made a great choice. But you don't know how the sales candidate you rejected would have done. Imagine that you found out later that she had been hired by your main competitor and was far outselling the salesperson *you* had hired: how would you feel about your decision?

Temporality: Vantage Points in Time

The costs and benefits of most decisions accrue over time, altering the nature of the outcome. A Taoist story of the farmer whose horse ran away illustrates this point. After the horse disappears, the neighbor arrives to console the farmer for the loss. The farmer replies philosophically: "Who knows what is good or bad?" A few days later, the horse returns, leading a herd of wild horses into the farmer's pen. The neighbor now congratulates the farmer on his good fortune. Again the farmer says, "Who knows what is good or bad?" The following week, one of the horses kicks the farmer's son. The neighbor shakes his head, expressing sympathy. The farmer repeats his refrain: "Who knows what is good or bad?" A week later, the army stops by to conscript new soldiers. The son is passed over, due to his broken leg. This appears to be excellent news . . . but, at this point we've learned, like the neighbor, that is does not only matter what we know today but also what will be revealed tomorrow. Any streak of luck can turn into a curse; any unfortunate event can turn out to be a blessing. It all depends on the moment you choose to declare that a decision or an action taken in the past has reached its ultimate conclusion.

Consider the example of a Harvard University student who decides to drop out in his sophomore year to pursue his dream. Many parents would consider this a tale of a bad decision—unless we are talking about Bill Gates, that is. He ditched Harvard in his second year to pursue programming for an early version of the personal computer, joining forces with another equally gifted computer nerd, Paul Allen. Together, they created Microsoft. Gates returned to Harvard in 2007 to receive an honorary degree. With this retrospective knowledge, it's easy enough to declare that it would have been a big mistake for Gates to stay at Harvard, graduate with his class, and take a comfortable job at a large company, such as IBM or Digital Equipment Corporation (DEC). But what parent would have been happy about his or her child dropping out of Harvard when the future was still shrouded in uncertainty? We often have to wait a long time before we can really judge if a decision was smart, dumb, lucky, or somewhere in between.

Under this logic, the more time that has elapsed, the more data we should have to judge the quality of a decision. However, the longer view isn't always the richer and more accurate one. The wait itself can introduce its own biases, from memory distortions to additional factors affecting the outcome. An especially pernicious complication is what researchers call the survival bias. History tends to be written by the winners—or at least the survivors. The Darwinian sieve may leave us with a highly distorted long-term record.

For example, the band of traitors who pledged their fortune to break from Britain and create the United States is revered today as the Founding Fathers. But if the redcoats-versus-rebels skirmish had turned out differently, they would certainly never have acquired this epithet. Further, Benedict Arnold, a British collaborator whose name is now a byword for treason in the United States, would be celebrated as a patriot. Even recent history is clouded by the fact that failed decisions and actions may be poorly reflected in the statistical records or journalistic accounts. As we judge how well stocks versus bonds fared as investment alternatives over centuries, do we really fully count all the failed companies? When we celebrate successful entrepreneurs over time, do we properly remember those who tried and failed miserably?

Chance: As Opposed to Skill

Fate can have a strong hand in the outcomes of any decision, throwing our notions of skill—and fairness—to the wind. The intertwining tales of two Arctic explorers in the early 20th century provide an illustration. In 1926, Norwegian explorer Roald Amundsen and Italian aviator Umberto Nobile crossed the North Pole in the airship *Norge*. It was a smooth and flawless passage from Spitsbergen to Alaska, with Nobile at the helm. The aftermath was far more turbulent. The Italian dictator Mussolini urged Nobile to take full credit for the flight; Nobile and Amundsen each engaged in fierce battles for public recognition. Two years later, in 1928, Nobile repeated the journey—this time in an Italian plane, with an all-Italian crew. Their equipment was identical to that of the *Norge*; the pilot, Nobile, was now more experienced, having done the same journey once before. But the *Italia* crashed on the ice. The disaster was an international incident and prompted a global search-and-rescue effort. Despite the harsh words they had exchanged, loyal Amundsen joined the search effort for his nemesis. He lost his life in the process. Nobile, ironically, survived—but he never recovered his Arctic career. What role did mistakes, versus chance, play in this dramatic tale of two pilots?

Another story provides a more lighthearted example of the strong role of chance—and the blind eye people will turn to it, particularly if they believe in their own skill. The winner of a massive prize from the Spanish National Lottery was asked by a reporter about his strategy. He explained his secret: he had chosen a ticket ending with the number 48. Pressed for further details, the winner recounted that for seven nights, he had dreamed about the number seven. "Since seven times seven is 48, I then looked for that ticket."

This story proves several points, including an obvious one (you don't need to be good at math to win the lottery: as any fifth grader could tell you, seven times seven is 49!). Mainly, however, it shows how hard it is to argue with success—even when one's own reasoning is flawed and all the credit should go to Lady Fortune. Clearly, our desire to believe that we have control over our own fate makes it difficult for humans to separate chance from skill. Harvard psychologist Ellen Langer calls this phenomenon the "illusion of control."[18] When the state of Massachusetts changed its state lottery setup to allow buyers to choose their own number, they saw a marked increase in revenues. On an individual level, we see this same illusory belief enacted in everything from a tribe's belief that their rain dance has the power to influence the weather to a student's loyalty to a certain lucky sweater during final exams.

Even Fortune 100 companies may be guilty of rain dances of their own, like engaging in sophisticated risk management and planning exercises that instill a sense of control while still missing their targets by a country mile. This bias to overestimate how much control our actions actually *had* is a huge barrier to our ability to judge, after the fact, to what extent the outcome of our decision or action was due to luck or skill.

Treatment Effects: Confounding Influences Ex Post Facto

A manager hires a new employee. It's a difficult decision—a number of qualified candidates had emerged, and her peers questioned her choice. She worries that she might have chosen incorrectly, so she invests extra time in the new hire. With her coaching, he proves to be a great success. Was her choice to hire him "brilliant"? Or did her coaching and other actions after the choice influence the outcome?

Researchers refer to actions taken after the decision as "treatment effects." These actions can be deliberate or hidden and inadvertent. The placebo effect in medicine is a well-known example. As countless studies have shown, the sheer belief in a drug's powers can influence its efficacy; some researchers estimate that placebo effects can be credited with up to one-third of the positive impact of certain drugs.[19] Self-fulfilling prophecies are common in life, such as economists making predictions about GNP growth which then influence business and consumer spending. Consider marriage or the choice of a life partner. Twenty years after making this monumental decision, you might conclude that you chose brilliantly—or that you chose in error. You try to reflect on your original choice and either congratulate yourself on your own good judgment or chide yourself for quelling your original doubts. But can you really go back in time and second-guess your decision? It will be impossible to ignore the many influences that your actions or those of your partner had on your lives over the intervening years.

A famous study in the field of industrial psychology, the Hawthorne effect, provides a classic example of both hidden treatment effects and brilliant discovery.[20] The Hawthorne Works was a large factory complex constructed by Western Electric in Cicero, Illinois, before the Second World War. About 45,000 workers, mainly women, built telephone equipment and consumer products such as refrigerators and fans. The facility was so enormous that it had its own private railroad. Considering the size of its operations, Hawthorne's management invested heavily in finding creative ways to elevate worker productivity, since even a difference of a few degrees could lead to major profits. Between 1924 and 1932, Elton Mayo and other Harvard researchers conducted a series of now famous experiments to study the impact of factory illumination. Initial results showed that even minute increases in illumination led to increased productivity. This was a stunning result. If better lighting really led to higher output, there would be major ramifications for factory design, at Hawthorne and across the country. But then the researchers noticed a curious condition: the effects of the lighting seemed to erode. Over time, workers' output slowed to the original rate of productivity. Even more curiously, when illumination was reduced to its old level, productivity rose as well. How, then, to account for the rise in output?

These puzzling results led to deep reflection. A subset of the Harvard professors, led by Fritz Roethlisberger and William J. Dickson, focused on a smaller group and conducted further experiments. They experimented with changing other factors and kept getting the same result: increased productivity. Interviews with the workers exposed the root cause: the impact was due not to the changes themselves but to the focused attention the workers received during the duration of the study. Apparently, workers' motivation increased in proportion to the attention that was paid to them. This key insight has yielded dividends far in excess of the cost of the original study. The Hawthorne studies catalyzed the human relations school of management, an era of management theory premised on the idea that each of us arrives at work with deep reserves of untapped potential. Over time, this approach has given rise to notions such as participative management, empowerment, quality control circles, and managers as cheerleaders—all of which would have seemed transgressive, even revolutionary, in previous eras.

The Hawthorne example is a powerful illustration of a brilliant mistake. Researchers began with an initial theory that led to puzzling empirical results. They did not deem the effort a waste of time, however—instead, they strove for deeper insight. The researchers sought new data, asked probing questions, and challenged their initial assumptions. These elements were all necessary to bring about the breakthrough insight. Workers are not machines; there is no magic bullet that will increase their productivity. Instead, they are motivated by complex psychological needs and desires. They enjoy having attention paid to their work: this alone increases their motivation and their output. Once this seminal insight was pried loose, the world of management would never be the same.

Missing Data: The Road Not Taken

Two roads diverged in a wood, and I—
I took the one less traveled by,
And that has made all the difference.
—ROBERT FROST, "The Road Not Taken"[21]

These lines are the conclusion of Frost's popular, widely anthologized "The Road Not Taken." The poem describes a moment of deliberation when a person walking through the woods notices two alternative paths and takes the one that seems less trodden. The final line, "And that has made all the difference," implies that this choice had monumental significance—not just for this journey but for the person's life as a whole. Let's compare this to a far more lowbrow example: a direct-mail pitch that the *Wall Street Journal* used to send out a few decades ago, before the rise of the Internet. In this pitch, the *Journal* told the story of two young managers—a subscriber and a nonsubscriber. The subscriber had access to all the latest information, parlaying it into a career of success and leadership. The nonsubscriber trailed in his wake. The message was clear: it would be foolish not to shell out a few bucks for a subscription.

It might seem jarring to juxtapose a beautiful poem and a simple advertisement. But each illustrates one of the essential dilemmas of judging mistakes. Both the Frost poem and the *Wall Street Journal* pitch are premised on the same idea: that a single choice can have consequential outcomes for the individual—and, further, that it's possible, without a doubt, to look at the past and to say, *Yes, I did make the right decision.* But here's the problem with this premise: there is often no way to tell where the other path—the one not chosen—would have taken us. In life, as opposed to art or advertisements, we are rarely confronted with clear, binary decision points. In fact, on many given days of our lives, we may ignore the choices in front of us rather than making active decisions. As the Buddha said, "There are two mistakes one can make along the road to truth—not going all the way, and not starting."[22]

The dread of making mistakes can lead to another type of error—that of failing to decide. At the end of their lives, people often regret the things they did not do as much as the things they did. They wish they had taken the other road, tried something different, corrected a past mistake, or improved a bad situation at work or at home. In Catholic theology, there are sins of commission and omission. Sins of commission are obvious: you do something you shouldn't do. Omission is far more subtle. You see the person being mugged on the street and don't call the police. Were you in the wrong, or did you simply not comprehend the full situation in time to act? For all of their subtlety, sins of omission are also difficult to catch (with the notable exception of a failure to file your tax return). Nevertheless, failing to act can have disastrous consequences.[23] The tragedy of genocide, for example, may be due as much to sins of omission (people turn their heads away, failing to protect the innocent) as to sins of commission (the killing itself).

Considering omitted alternatives can lead to some tricky philosophical debates. After all, Frost's walker in the woods can't *really* know how life would have evolved if the other path had been taken. Furthermore, no matter which path we choose, there is always further divergence and variation. So two travelers on the same path—regardless of whether they have a subscription to the *Wall Street Journal*—can have completely different experiences.

Sometimes, however, it *is* possible to see "the road not taken"—or at least, some key elements of it. You should be able to monitor the progress of stocks that you did not buy (although few of us do). Or that first love you allowed to slip through your fingers in high school might have dated or married your friend. This can give you some sense of how an alternate decision might have played out, although not necessarily how your own case would have evolved, given the complexity of decisions and interactions with others. As far as possible, we need to consider all of the available data in judging mistakes and, at the same time, recognize that decision making is often a dynamic, evolving process.

Who Makes the Call?

Legendary baseball umpire Bill Klem once faced an irate player demanding that he call a pitch. "Is it a ball or strike?" the player asked. Klem took his time, replying slowly: "Sonny, it ain't nothing till I call it."[24] In real life, as opposed to baseball, it's not always clear who gets to make the final call about mistakes.

Klem's reply raises an ontological dilemma: before the umpire makes the call, does a "ball" or a "strike" even exist?— or is it simply a construct, a creation of the umpire's judgment? Mistakes don't exist as objective entities; like a ball or a strike, the difference does not exist until the decision has been declared by the individual with the power to make the call. The salient question this raises is: who is or should be the "umpire" of the mistake? How does that person's opinion and view affect what others consider to be true? Baseball has clear rules that make this plain—the umpire, of course, is the person in the gray pants, agnostic to either team's agenda— but in real life, there is no such thing as an unbiased external arbiter. There is no umpire for the mistakes we make in life, even if they land us in a court of law. This ambiguity about who decides, and when the judgment is made, introduces a major element of subjectivity into the definition of a mistake. Ultimately, a mistake is in the eye of the beholder. This important realization should make readers less afraid of making mistakes, especially the kind that will in due time prove to be beneficial ones, or perhaps even brilliant.

It isn't simple to define a mistake. The process by which a decision was made can be as relevant as the outcome—and in real life, both can be hard to pin down. As we've seen through the examples in this chapter, a "bad" outcome can be due to a faulty decision process, random chance, or someone's interference with the process after the initial decision was made. Moreover, depending on the point in time at which we assess the nature of the outcomes and *who* makes this determination, a decision can appear in a very different light.

What's the purpose of walking through all of this complexity? First and foremost, since I will later argue that some mistakes are worth making, it helps to start with a clear definition of *mistakes* and a shared understanding of the biases that arise when we use the term. If you are a manager who wants to champion greater risk taking and introduce the idea of mistakes as undervalued portals of innovation in your organization, you'll need to recognize the multiple factors that will conspire to complicate this effort. You will need to work hard to reframe common misperceptions about mistakes. Finally, you'll need to introduce yardsticks for measuring mistakes that recognize the role of chance and treatment effects and exercise sagacious judgment about who gets to make the final call.

CHAPTER 2

Not All Errors Are Equal
Brilliant Mistakes

Success is 99% failure.
—SAICHIRO HONDA, FOUNDER, HONDA MOTOR COMPANY[25]

In the previous chapter, I defined a mistake as a decision that's less than optimal, given what could reasonably have been known at the time of choice. In this chapter, I go a step further and define the paradoxical notion of a *brilliant* mistake—one that surprises us with outcomes that far outweigh the cost.

At first, the idea of a brilliant mistake might seem oxymoronic. But, as this chapter shows, not all mistakes are created equal. Some have the potential to rise above their costly beginnings and yield dividends far beyond the original investment. Brilliance can occur before as well as after a mistake: in the conditions that lead up to it and the new insights that emerge in its wake. As we'll see, successful inventors and leaders often create conditions that, over time, lead to productive mistakes. They generate their own luck by orchestrating circumstances where chance and insight coincide with spark.

Mistakes with Potential

Let's start with a striking example. In the winter of 1961, Edward Lorenz, an academic meteorologist, made a very small mistake with remarkable long-term consequences. Lorenz was working on weather prediction models using computer simulation, a common tool of his trade. This was the era of the mainframe computer, when simulations required detailed program instruction, punch cards, batch processing, and hard copy printouts. From soup to nuts, each simulation could take hours, and computer time was expensive. One fateful day, Lorenz had just completed a large round of simulations of a particular weather system and wanted to repeat the experiment over a longer time frame. Rather than waste valuable processing time, he used the printout from the first simulation run and manually typed in final numbers from the results table. In other words, to be efficient, he simply picked up where the previous run had left off.

The results of the second simulation diverged radically from Lorenz's expectation. Like the good scientist he was, Lorenz backtracked, looking for where he must have gone astray. Perhaps he had typed in a wrong number—or maybe the computer itself had malfunctioned. He puzzled about it for days. Then it struck him: he had entered numbers using a computer printout that rounded all numbers to three places of precision after the decimal. In the computer's memory, however, numbers were stored to six decimal places of precision. For example, the number stored might be 4896.506127, but the computer printout on paper would read 4896.506. By entering the numbers by hand, Lorenz had changed them ever so slightly. This tiny rounding error of 0.000127 in the initial conditions pushed the second simulation onto quite a different path, with vastly different weather results. Lorenz had made a small mistake with large, unforeseen consequences.

At this point, it was clear to Lorenz that the rounding error had thrown off his original model. Most researchers would have stopped there, accepted defeat, and gone in another direction. But Lorenz continued to reflect on the odd result. He was struck by the idea that small changes in a complex system with nonlinear feedback loops could yield such tremendous consequences. As he put in a 1972 presentation to the American Association for the Advancement of Science: "Does the flap of a butterfly's wings in Brazil set off a tornado in Texas?" The answer is yes—small changes in complex systems can snowball and magnify the initial deviation. Although the original weather prediction program he had designed had failed in its intent, its result led Lorenz to a far more significant discovery: what's now known as the "butterfly effect." Lorenz has assumed an honored place in science as the father of chaos theory. He was awarded the 1991 Kyoto Prize for discovering "deterministic chaos." The prize committee noted that Lorenz's principle had "profoundly influenced a wide range of basic sciences and brought about one of the most dramatic changes in mankind's view of nature since Sir Isaac Newton." It touched on such deep issues as whether the universe is deterministic or stochastic, a debate harking back to Heisenberg's uncertainty principle in physics and Einstein's famous remark that God does not play dice with the universe.

Lorenz's profound insight shook the foundations of science. A rounding error turned into a brilliant mistake. If Lorenz hadn't put in the truncated numbers, he never would have been faced with an unexpected result. If he hadn't recognized the implications of this result, thanks to extensive training, keen observation, and dogged pursuit of possible explanations, he wouldn't have developed chaos theory. This example illustrates the two prime ingredients of a brilliant mistake:

1. something goes wrong far beyond the range of prior expectation; and
2. new insights emerge whose benefits greatly exceed the mistake's cost.

The brilliant part lies especially in condition (2), but also in recognizing that (1) is necessary for (2) to occur. In later chapters, I demonstrate that our actions should aim to increase the chance of (1) and (2) occurring together. If those two conditions are met, we are dealing with a brilliant mistake.

Inventors, or Professional Mistake Makers?

Clearly, mistakes are often the source of new insights. Almost any invention story illustrates this fact. Thomas Edison's famous discovery of the lightbulb was not a flash of brilliance but the end result of a tedious strategy of repeated testing. Before he discovered that a carbonized thread could serve as a lightbulb filament, Edison tested hundreds of other materials, including platinum and other metals. When he failed on his 700th try, he was asked why he didn't give up. He replied, "I have not failed 700 times; I've discovered 700 things that do not work." He was aware, in other words, that *productive mistakes* were a part of his process. In October of 1879, Edison hit his first level of success: a filament that would burn for 13.5 hours. He continued to improve this design; by November 1879, he filed for a US patent for an electric lamp using "a carbon filament or strip coiled and connected . . . to platinum contact wires."[26] Several months after the patent was granted, his team discovered that a carbonized bamboo filament could last over 1,200 hours.

A more recent example is that of Sir James Dyson, inventor of the radical new bagless vacuum cleaner that swept away the market. Over 15 years of failures, Dyson pounded through 5,127 prototypes. He described his process to *Fast Company*: "There were 5,126 failures. But I learned from each one." He continued, "We're taught to do things the right way. But if you want to discover something that other people haven't, you need to do things the wrong way." Surely Edison would have agreed. As Dyson noted, in our society, "we admire instant brilliance, effortless brilliance. I think quite the reverse. You should admire the person who perseveres and slogs through and gets there in the end."[27]

Questioning Assumptions

Mistakes can make us wiser. The great virtue of a mistake, whether accidental or by design, is its ability to puncture bubbles of false beliefs and open up new vistas. As such, we should embrace mistakes as portals of discovery that reach beyond our normal channels of observations.

History demonstrates how ideas that we now consider patently false were once accepted wisdom. In his pioneering study *The American Soldier* (1949–1950), sociologist Paul Lazarsfeld used rigorous empirical research to demonstrate the falsehood of numerous ideas that people deemed true beyond question—such as the belief that racially integrated platoons were less effective.[28] Lazarsfeld's study shattered many erroneous beliefs and became a landmark in the field of sociology. Good science challenges received wisdom with empirical data and better theory. A 2009 book, *50 Great Myths of Popular Psychology*, examines numerous commonly accepted myths about the ways our minds function. Using up-to-date evidence from scientific literature, the book debunks many popular misconceptions, such as the belief that most people use only 10 % of their brainpower, the idea that low self-esteem causes psychological problems, and the view that hypnosis is a "trance" state that differs radically from wakefulness.[29] Through careful deconstruction of each of these ideas, the book also presents insights about why certain erroneous ideas gain such a powerful hold through sheer repetition in the popular media or in our social circles.

Consider, for instance, the idea that bicycle helmets keep us safe by protecting riders from head injuries. This idea has, in general, attained the veracity of accepted wisdom. Many

American states and cities have instituted helmet laws; the state of Pennsylvania, for example, has required children under 12 to wear helmets since 1995. But *is* it really always true that helmets make us safer? Some cyclists argue that wearing a helmet might make them *more likely* to be hit by a car. Ian Walker, an avid cyclist and psychologist at the University of Bath, put the question to a test. He rigged the bicycle he rides to work with an ultrasonic sensor. For two months, he rode with or without a helmet, using his sensor to measure the berth given to him by passing cars. His discovery was surprising. As reported in the March 2007 issue of *Accident Analysis & Prevention*, when Walker wore his helmet, drivers edged an average of 3.35 inches closer to him. Critics suggested that the difference was small compared to the wide berth vehicles give to cyclists, so Walker reanalyzed the data. He found that vehicles were 23% more likely to move within the one-meter "danger zone" around him when he was wearing his helmet.

Walker went further in his counterintuitive study. On some of his test rides, he donned a long brown wig. His intent was for passing motorists to mistake him for a woman. This protection, he found, granted him an additional layer of protection—specifically, an average of 2.2 more inches of breathing room. We can only speculate about the reasons for this gender effect, from greater courtesy shown to females to a prejudice about women being less steady on their bikes. Whatever the reason, according to Walker's study, cyclists would be well served by adorning their helmets with long, flowing locks.

While Walker's results remain controversial, they illustrate how tacit assumptions and common beliefs (for example, "helmet-riders are safer") can be incorrect.[30] In the event of a crash, a helmet inarguably provides a rider with additional protection. However, if we also consider the likelihood of a crash, and the manner in which drivers' imperfect judgments affect the rider's safety, the helmet's protective power might be significantly reduced—perhaps even reversed. The experiment highlights how the complexity of a real-life situation can make it difficult to declare, without reservation, that *any* assumption is 100% certain. Since we use flawed assumptions to judge whether a decision is right or wrong—right to wear a helmet, wrong not to wear one—we cannot tell whether the assumptions themselves are correct until we make a mistake. By doing the wrong thing, we may gain the knowledge needed to be more right in the future.

I was born and raised in the Netherlands, where we have many canals. In most countries, it is presumed that wearing a safety belt is the best way to protect the occupants of a car. In Amsterdam, however, with its quaint canals and cobblestone streets, many poor souls have perished when their cars toppled into the canal and the seat belt kept the passengers from freeing themselves in time.

Humans have a tendency to seek confirming evidence. We focus on explanations and data that support our beliefs and glide over alternative explanations. Consider your own habits—are you likely to consult articles or news shows that support your political opinions, or do you seek out strong counterarguments to try to test and revisit them? Scientists are not exempt from this trap.

Consider the story of NASA's effort to settle the debates about the moon's origin by distributing moon rocks to various laboratories for analysis. Through this distribution, NASA had hoped that a scientific consensus would emerge. To their dismay, the opposite happened. After carefully studying the rocks, applying the highest standards of scientific objectivity, each research group returned to NASA more convinced than ever that its own theory was correct. Somehow, with identical evidence, each lab managed to conduct analyses protecting its researchers' existing theories and buttressing its established positions.

The NASA story raises some troubling doubts about the very notion of scientific objectivity. It also suggests why the confirmation bias often leads to faulty conclusions and why mistakes may be our only salvation. Imagine if NASA were to return to those labs and ask each to conduct analysis that somehow contradicted their original beliefs. The labs might then explore pieces of the data that they had previously discarded as outliers or mistakes. Such a process could resolve the deadlock between labs and help create scientific consensus.

I used this approach when consulting with a well-known pharmaceutical company that was concerned about the high rate of experimental drugs that were getting through their phase 1 trials. Because just a tiny fraction of compounds tested will make it into the market as drugs, pharmaceutical manufacturers are eager to find methods for rejecting the "bad" ones as soon as possible. Phase 1, then, ought to be designated as the "killing fields" for compounds that are unlikely ever to reach the market. However, most of the scientists involved in the decision process will favor the compounds they are researching, just as the NASA scientists were invested in defending their own lab's cherished theory. I proposed a role reversal. We asked the scientists and review committee who were responsible for screening compounds to design clinical tests aimed at proving that the compound would likely fail. This approach resulted in different test design, focusing less on potential benefit and more on toxicity or other side effects. The approach also identified interactions with other drugs a patient might take sooner, as well as additional risks that under the old approach would emerge only in later test phases.

It proved highly beneficial to this pharmaceutical company to find evidence that countered initial assumptions and hopes. As we'll examine in later chapters, contradicting established beliefs is a proven method to get to the right answers sooner. The key is to approach any complex inquiry with the right mind-set, one that balances confirming thinking with disconfirmation. The less we know about the problem at hand, the more we need disconfirmation to weed out false hypotheses quickly. As we warn our PhD students, if you torture the data set long enough, it will confess. Without disconfirmation, we fall into the trap of running only experiments aimed at proving our initial hypothesis and deluding ourselves along the way.

Types of Errors, and Their Relative Benefits

There will never be a shortage of dumb mistakes. *Fortune* magazine once compiled a list of doozies, including Merrill Lynch's investment in subprime mortgages just before the market meltdown in 2008, Mattel's recall of 20 million toys treated in China with lead paint, and the fines a Rhode Island Hospital faced for operating on the wrong side of a patient's head for the third time in less than a year.[31] The annual Darwin Awards have raised fatal error analysis to a macabre ritual. Each year, they award a posthumous award to people who died as a result of their own foolish mistakes; these mistakes, they argue, "chlorinate the gene pool" or "cull the herd." Examples include a hunter who died after shooting himself following an altercation with his dog and a priest who perished trying to reach heaven in helium-filled balloons.

Let's look politely away from these true outlier cases of natural selection and concentrate on mistakes of the more fruitful kind. The following framework can assist you in distinguishing different types of mistakes using simple cost-benefit analysis. The vertical axis of figure 2-1 charts the relative costs of a mistake, from low to high, while the horizontal axis charts the relative benefits of the mistake, again from low to high. This allows us to group mistakes into four "types," with some illustrative examples:

A) Tragic (high cost, low benefit): driving car into tree and being badly injured

B) Serious (high cost, high benefit): getting a divorce; filing for bankruptcy

C) Trivial (low cost, low benefit): getting a parking ticket; losing your wallet

D) Brilliant (low cost, high benefit): Lorenz discovering the butterfly effect

Fig 2-1 The 4 Types of Mistakes

Potential Benefits of the Mistake?

		Low	High
Costs of the Mistake?	High	**A. Tragic Mistakes** - Fatal car crash - Drug addiction	**B. Serious Mistakes** - Getting divorced - New venture failing
	Low	**C. Trivial Mistakes** - Parking ticket - Missing a plane	**D. Brilliant Mistakes** - Lab error ▸ discovery - Losing job ▸ new career

Clearly, tragic mistakes (A), which exact a high price with little personal benefit, are to be wholly avoided. Serious mistakes (B) also have a high cost, but with the potential of a high benefit—such as getting a divorce or failing in a business venture. These mistakes can provide tremendous lessons and may be valuable in retrospect, but we need to be careful about inviting them into our lives. You shouldn't get divorced to see what you will learn; you don't drive your business into the ground to taste the lessons of failure. A third class, trivial mistakes (C), represent low cost and low reward. Examples of these are getting a parking ticket or missing a plane. The results are not tragic, but the lessons learned are inconsequential or obvious—along the lines of "put more money in the meter" or "leave for the airport a bit earlier."

Distinguishing between these types allows us to arrive at a more tangible definition of the truly brilliant mistakes (D)—those that offer high benefits at a relatively low cost. As the stories so far illustrate, the high benefits of brilliant mistakes typically accrue over the long run rather than being conferred at the instant of the error. This is part of what makes them difficult to distinguish from trivial, or even serious, errors. It would be tempting to look at this chart and determine, "Well, I guess I'll try to make only brilliant mistakes, then!" The real lesson, however, is that these distinctions are often clear only in retrospect.

For example, some major flops in business only later turned into big successes, such as McDonald's Hula Burger (1962), Apple's Lisa (1983), Coca Cola's New Coke (1985), or Corning's DNA Microarray (1998).[32] While it's important to live and work within the boundaries of good sense (none of us want to end up immortalized as the next Darwin Award winner!), it's also true that striving to eliminate all mistakes in our lives means that we risk sacrificing valuable ones as well. We need to allow some of the bad errors into our lives in order to have a decent chance of creating some brilliant mistakes as well. That is the challenge: how best to manage this trade-off based on your ambition and risk tolerance.

To summarize, this chapter explored several important aspects of mistakes:

1. **Not all mistakes are bad.** As Lorenz found, the mistake in his experiment propelled him in the direction of a powerful new idea. Mistakes get a bad rap at times. We believe that they are to be avoided at all costs. But progress actually occurs in fits and starts, failures and successes. Mistakes allow us to learn more quickly and take us in new directions. Some mistakes are very bad, but others lead to brilliance. As we'll discuss later, mistakes speed learning and expand options.

2. **It is easy to dismiss that which seems out of your control.** The bias to overestimate how much control we have greatly complicates the task of judging after the fact whether a good or bad outcome was due to luck or skill. If Lorenz had believed that some poltergeist had shifted his data, he would never have recognized the fundamentally new principle that led to chaos theory. But rather than attribute the error to random noise or bad luck, he explored it further and found a path from this apparent cul-de-sac to genius.

3. **Mistakes don't happen in a vacuum.** After we make a decision, we continue to perform actions that influence outcomes. The placebo effect in medicine, whereby a patient improves simply because he believes in the power of his medicine, is one well-known example. Self-fulfilling prophecies are common in life, such as economists making gloomy predictions and thereby delaying recovering. Also, they can be subtle, such as parents or teachers unconsciously enacting their beliefs about a child and thereby influencing the outcome. Sometimes bad decisions can become good simply through concerted or indirect effort.

4. **Brilliant mistakes have two prime ingredients.** They require that: *(1) something go wrong far beyond the range of prior expectation and (2) this allows for deep new insights to emerge whose benefits far exceed the cost of the original mistake.* The brilliant human part lies especially in (2) but also in recognizing that (1) is necessary for (2). The trick is to engage in actions that increase the chance of (1) and (2) occurring together.

Once we recognize that not all mistakes are equal, the challenge becomes which ones to encourage and which to suppress. Brilliant mistakes can be viewed as buying options, akin to financial call options, because you incur a small cost now in order to have an opportunity to learn and earn more later. But unlike real options, brilliant mistakes cannot be easily modeled or optimized ahead of time because you are operating at the boundary of your knowledge. Moreover, if you did look at them analytically, brilliant mistakes would end up with a negative expected return and would be rejected by most of your colleagues. It requires an element of intuition, as well as an attitude favorable toward testing your thinking at deeper levels than can be rationally justified. Since intuition can be deeply flawed, it is also important to avoid dumb mistakes, as examined next.

CHAPTER 3

Why and How We Err
Causes and Remedies

*Men occasionally stumble over the truth, but most of them
pick themselves up and hurry off as if nothing had happened.*
—WINSTON CHURCHILL

The goal of this chapter is to help you understand, and
thereby move beyond, your resistance to learning from
mistakes. Using an example from the legal system, we'll inves-
tigate how cognitive and emotional forces can conspire to
suppress the truth. This, in turn, will position you to learn
from mistakes and prepare you for the preposterous idea I
propose in the following chapter—an approach for making
deliberate mistakes.

Developing a Forensic Mind-set

In the 1960s, the mathematician John Stallings published a
proof of Poincare's conjecture. The theorem concerned a
deep math problem that had occupied the best minds for
centuries. It conjectured that any finite shape that does not
have holes can be stretched and deformed into a sphere.
Stallings proved the theorem for seven dimensions and
higher, opening broad new vistas in the world of mathematics. Later, in a famous 1965 paper ironically titled "How Not
to Prove the Poincare Conjecture," he retracted his proof and
explained how and why he had erred.

Science, as a field, accepts that ideas evolve through the
proof and subsequent disproof of alternative theories. It was
not unusual (or shameful) that Stallings proposed an idea

that was later proved wrong, although in mathematics you do want to get it right the first time. Nonetheless, in publishing a flawed proof, Stallings helped contribute to the eventual resolution of Poincare's conjecture. As Harvard mathematician Barry Mazur noted: "This is a very, very deep geometric problem; different proofs bring out different aspects of the problem." What *was* unique was Stallings's willingness to publicly declare, and claim, his own error. With humility and good humor, he described the "blindness" that led to his false conclusion—the way that irrational forces, like excitement and fear of being wrong, occluded his vision. He wrote, "I was unable to find flaws in my 'proof' for quite a while. It was a psychological problem, a blindness, an excitement, an inhibition of reasoning by an underlying fear of being wrong."[33]

Few of us like to make mistakes. They are a vivid—and often painful—reminder of our limitations, our fallibility. Consequently, after a mistake, most of us simply move on, eager to sweep the error under the carpet. Rather than extract hidden lessons, we try to protect our bruised egos, control the damage, and concoct reasons why others were to blame. But turning ordinary mistakes into brilliant ones requires the opposite approach. Like Stallings continuing to probe his theorem for holes or Lorenz, in the previous chapter, poring over his data to find the real story behind his puzzling results, you need to focus on your own error, seeking the deeper meaning. In order to understand the bigger picture, you need a forensic mind-set and a willingness to put your own ego aside. Only then will Mother Nature reveal her deeper secrets. This is not easy, especially when we are at the painful side of failure.

Innocent Mistakes

On September 30, 1979, tragedy struck Dianna and Kevin Green. Dianna, pregnant with the couple's first child, was attacked in their apartment. Her severe injuries led to the loss of the child. She also lost almost all memory of the incident and the ability to speak. Kevin Green told the police that Dianna had been alone in the apartment during the attack. An employee at a local fast-food restaurant confirmed his alibi, and his take-out food was still warm when the police arrived. But the couple had a history of arguments that had intensified during her pregnancy. Although she continued to suffer from brain damage and amnesia, Dianna testified against her husband. On October 2, 1980, Kevin was convicted of second-degree murder for the death of the unborn fetus and attempted murder of his wife.

Clearly, this story is about a mistake with devastating consequences. It is *not*, however, the story of Kevin's mistake, but of errors in the legal system that convicted him. After 16 years in prison, new DNA evidence emerged that proved Dianna's attacker to be Gerald Parker, a convicted serial killer. Parker confessed to the attack on Dianna, as well as five other murders.[34] The *real* mistakes had been made by law enforcement and prosecutors, and these mistakes cost Green 16 years of his life and allowed a dangerous criminal to roam free. In October 1999, California governor Gray Davis awarded Kevin Green $620,000 in compensation for his wrongful conviction. This sad story is one of more than 200 such cases successfully pursued by the Innocence Project, a nonprofit movement involving law school students and professors. The aim is to identify erroneous convictions using new techniques of DNA testing and reform the criminal justice system to prevent further injustice. It's possible that cases like Kevin's are just the tip of the iceberg since DNA testing is available for only about 10% of all violent crimes.[35] There may be thousands of inmates in prison for crimes they did not commit, lacking any clear-cut ways of proving their innocence.

With so much at stake, how can such devastating mistakes happen—particularly in a system like the judicial process, with its rigorous checks and balances? Theoretically, the American justice system is structured to determine, beyond the shadow of a doubt, whether individuals accused of crimes are guilty. In criminal cases especially, the bar for proof is set high. As Supreme Court Justice Blackmun once declared, it is worse to convict one innocent person than to let ten guilty people off the hook. In practice, however, if the standard is too high, there would be few convictions, and many guilty perpetrators would remain free. This creates pressures that can lead to wrongful convictions, which seem to be all too common.

Drowning in a Pool of Subjectivity

Why do serious mistakes occur in a system designed to vet the evidence, argue the case from multiple angles, and abide by clear rules of evidence? How can decision-making entities that are theoretically without bias—an independent jury and an impartial judge—come to erroneous conclusions?

First, the data may not be reliable. Eyewitness reports and other commonly used data can easily corrupt or distort evidence. A study by Brandon Garrett, a law professor at the University of Virginia, examined 200 cases of wrongful convictions, all of which were overturned based on DNA evidence. The study identified a number of common factors:

- **Faulty eyewitness evidence.** The leading cause was erroneous evidence by eyewitnesses, a problem in 79% of overturned cases. Stress distorts memories, particularly visual ones: under duress, few people remember accurately what happened around them, especially when dealing with shocking events like assaults or even car accidents. According to research by Elizabeth Loftus, witnesses may swear to something that they didn't actually see at least 50% of the time.[36] Nevertheless, jurors treat eyewitness accounts as objective.

- **Faulty forensic evidence.** This factor played a role in 55% of the cases of overturned convictions. Forensic evidence—such as hair samples, blood, or semen, and DNA—can lend an air of impartiality to legal proceedings because it is presumably scientific. But often such evidence can be tainted, misinterpreted, or even outright manipulated, as the bloody glove in the infamous O. J. Simpson murder trial made clear.

- **Unreliable informant testimony.** In 18% of overturned cases, informant testimony was a part of the prosecution's case, and informants can be highly motivated to lie. In many cases, the informant was later found guilty of the accused crime; alternatively, he or she may have testified falsely to get a lesser sentence or early parole for another violation. This factor differs from the other factors since it entails a conscious attempt to create bias (on the part of the witness if not the prosecution); the earlier factors cited operate largely subconsciously.

These factors highlight a tragic element of the human mind and its ability to confuse suggestive impressions with absolute certainty. As the sad Kevin Green case makes plain, an original mistake—in his case, his initial arrest—can be compounded by layer upon layer of subsequent errors, attributable to factors as divergent as bad data (like faulty forensic evidence) and the sheer unreliability of human minds. In addition to information distortions, there are other sources of mistakes. Flawed jury processes and the pitfalls of group processes such as groupthink can lead to errors.[37]

There is pressure on police and prosecutors to convict someone for a high-profile crime. This pressure can lead to a
confirmation bias. Officers may have a hunch about a certain
suspect and then suppress evidence that doesn't fit while
highlighting the details that do. This chain of mistakes can
lead to a miscarriage of justice, with much agony for the
innocent victims involved.[38]

It might seem naïve to find hope in a story as depressing
as Kevin Green's. But the high incidence of false convictions
revealed by DNA evidence has the potential to strengthen our
legal rules and procedures. Recognizing errors and exploring
their roots are the first steps toward brilliant mistakes. Eventually the work of individuals and organizations like the Innocence Project will lead to better procedures for interpreting
evidence and meting out justice. This will benefit thousands
of criminally accused persons who have yet to be tried on serious charges. If so, the wrongful convictions of the past are
providing the seeds of brilliant new insights and procedures.

The Innocence Project example shows how a confluence
of factors can interrupt the flow of justice and how human
fallibility can thwart the ability to see the truth or make fair
decisions. It's helpful to define common factors that can stand
in the way of our ability to clearly see and understand mistakes.

Emotional Factors

Various emotional barriers prevent us from dwelling on
mistakes. It is *much* more satisfying to be right than wrong!
Even when alone, we may derive pleasure from correctly
calling a coin toss or the outcome of a football game, and
become chagrined when we make a wrong turn in traffic or
get stuck in a crossword puzzle. Social settings magnify these
private feelings. It is a bitter pill to hear another say, "I told
you so"; conversely, it often tastes sweet to dish out that
comment. Many expressions associated with mistakes high-

light its raw, visceral quality. We speak of people eating crow, humble pie, their hat, and of course their words. Mistakes are hard to digest and may literally make us sick to our stomach. As Kathryn Schulz states in her splendid book *Being Wrong: Adventures in the Margin of Error,* "If being right is succulent, being wrong runs a narrow, unhappy gamut from nauseating to worse than death."[39]

Not surprisingly, when we are wrong, various defense mechanisms, from cognitive dissonance and rationalization to denial, spring into action to protect our egos and reputations. When you make a false prediction or foolish decision, your mind enters a state of dissonance. On the one hand, you know that you've erred; on the other, you believe yourself to be a capable and smart individual. To reconcile these conflicting notions, you have two options: you can lower your self-view a notch or two, or you can rationalize—for instance, spin a story about why the mistake is not yours after all. Leon Festinger, a pioneering researcher in cognitive dissonance, conducted a classic experiment to observe, firsthand, the strategy of rationalization.[40]

Festinger infiltrated a religious cult whose leader had prophesied the end of the world. In anticipation of the event, the cult retreated to a high mountain to escape Armageddon; Festinger accompanied them to observe how they would react. When the world failed to end as predicted, there was initial surprise and disappointment. Clearly, the cult was in the throes of cognitive dissonance: how to resolve their faith in their leader with the actuality of the world's still being here? After some debate, the cult started to argue that their fervent prayers had actually saved the world. Their belief system proved immune to falsification; this was the defense mechanism the cult needed to survive. Although we can clearly see the cult's self-delusion, we are often engaged in similar behaviors. Our human capacity to deny reality should never be underestimated; it can afflict entire industries, countries, and cultures.[41]

Although our emotions can stand in the way of learning, they can also serve a positive role.[42] It is through intense feeling that we internalize life's hard-won lessons. A story of my own foolishness will demonstrate this point. I was in Europe, driving a diesel rental car. Having been born and raised in the Netherlands, I am well aware that a diesel car does not tolerate regular gasoline. I had scoffed at people who ruined their engines by putting in the wrong fuel, and I had seen countless tourists stranded beside the road due to this error. Late one night, I stopped my rental car in Belgium, just short of the French border, and I put a gasoline nozzle into the tank. In Holland, where I'd last filled the car, the nozzles are designed to be idiot-proof—a gasoline nozzle will not fit a diesel car—but Belgium does not afford these protections. Jet lag, the darkness of the late hour, and my overconfidence brought me to a slow but definite halt near a small village in France about 20 minutes later, with large lorries thundering by and no help in sight. After walking two kilometers in the dark to find a call box, communicating in broken French with a tow service, and waking a confused but helpful Avis rep, I finally managed to have the car returned to the rental outlet. I even found a taxi at 3:00 a.m. in that small village to drive me 140 kilometers to Paris so that I could give a 9:00 a.m. lecture (on the topic of critical thinking, no less).

This mistake had an impact: I felt foolish, and, for a few dark hours along the highway, I even feared for my life. I nearly missed my speaking engagement in Paris, lost a night of sleep, and later faced a $4,500 charge from Avis on my credit card bill. I assumed that the bill was for having ruined the engine. It was actually a mistake on their part: Avis thought I had never returned the car and billed me for over three months of renting in Europe. It all got straightened out in the end, and Avis even paid my taxi to Paris—*merci bien.*

Precisely because this mistake was deeply personal, it got my attention. I am highly unlikely to make such an error ever again. I also thought about selling better nozzles in Belgium to prevent others from being as stupid as I was. My moment of idiocy hit me in the head and the stomach, being stranded at midnight along a strange highway. Because this mistake hurt, it had more value than a mistake made by someone else. It prompted me to reflect, got me angry, and then motivated me to think about new business ideas. The school of hard knocks is a great teacher, even if the tuition is very high, precisely because the lessons make such a deep imprint. We need emotion born of direct, difficult experience to internalize, remember, and learn.

Cognitive Gaps

In addition to emotional obstacles, cognitive gaps can complicate learning in the real world. These include incomplete feedback, treatment effects, and confounded data. Learning from experience is a painstaking process that requires the discipline of scientific inquiry. We need careful experimentation, control groups, and double-blind studies to extract deeper insights from our complex world. To rise above the factors that conspire to obscure your search for truth, you must learn to recognize your own cognitive blind spots, tendencies such as wishful thinking, overconfidence, and selective perception.

Sometimes, allowing other people to pressure-test our thinking can help to shatter our delusions. In theory, group and organizational decisions should be less prone to error, because people can correct one another's false assumptions. In reality, however, groups can introduce their own biases—from groupthink to polarization—and these can undermine the benefit of different people's viewpoints. Furthermore, high intellect is no guardian against this tendency: some evidence even suggests that the smarter people are, the more tenacious they are about holding on to outdated ideas. As

Thomas Kuhn found, the acceptance of a new idea in science sometimes requires the passing of an entire generation of scientists trained in the "old school" of thought.[43] Once entrenched in the paradigms that made them successful, very few scientists can accept the new radical ideas of their "immature" graduate students (such as natural selection or quantum mechanics).

Beyond science, other fields and professions have been known to cling to false beliefs, even in the face of much counterevidence. Even systems especially designed with dialectic tension to bring out all viewpoints—such as in the case of Kevin Green—may still not conquer the foibles and quirks of the human mind. Many professional specialties have long lists of mistakes that are characteristic to that domain. Jerome Groopman's book *How Doctors Think* (2007) lays out various traps in the field of medicine; *Military Misfortunes* (1990) by Eliot Cohen and John Gooch does so for the battlefield. Charles Kindleberger's classic book *Manias, Panics, and Crashes* (1978) recounts lessons from many centuries of financial crises. In *Inside the Jury* (1983), Reid Hastie et al offer a peek into the tangled and flawed thinking of jurors. These books are good starting points to help you strategize about where the system you operate in is most biased.

The subject of human error has been studied widely in such fields as psychology, sociology, economics, and philosophy. As noted in the preface, the 2002 Nobel Prize in Economics was awarded for cognitive science research pioneered by Daniel Kahneman and Amos Tversky.[44] This stream of research documents the many ways in which ordinary humans can depart from rational judgment and choice in daily life. A synopsis of this vast field is beyond our scope, but the model shown in figure 3-1 provides a summary of key phases underlying a decision process.[45] The most important phase is listed in the center of the diagram and is termed the meta-decision. It is about making sure that you are solving the right problem. Here we ask what the crux of the problem is, who should be involved in its resolution, and what key traps or biases to avoid. Once the meta-decision has been settled, the other four phases can be tackled.

Fig 3-1 Phases of the Decision Process

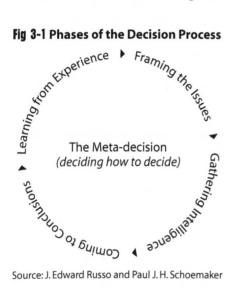

Source: J. Edward Russo and Paul J. H. Schoemaker

The 4 Key Phases in Decision Making

The decision process can be conceptualized as consisting of the four phases shown as arrows in figure 3-1. Although we discuss them in sequence, in real life they are less linear. Insights from one phase can influence another. For example, intelligence gathering may lead you to reframe the original decision or even revisit the meta-decision. Likewise, deeper thought about the coming-to-conclusion phase may lead you to collect more data or revise your frame.

Phase 1: Decision Framing

This key phase is about mental structure we impose on the problem: what objectives we should pursue, which options are available to us, and what constraints exist. It also includes the time frame of the decision, the scope of the problem, which yardsticks to use to measure success, and what reference points to use. For example, many firms use past performance, or that of close competitors, as the reference point for judging success. Such myopic framing plagued the automobile industry in Detroit throughout the 1970s and Sears in the 1980s. The real competition came from elsewhere, such as oversea rivals for Detroit and new media (QVC) for Sears. Also, managers often compare new ideas against the status quo. But this reference point ignores that the status quo is not static and may get worse due to competition, new regulations, and so on. To avoid this trap, Ford Motor Company often required that the status quo option (doing nothing) receive the same scrutiny and longer-term justification as other options.

In the framing phase it is critical to challenge assumptions and think outside the box. Consider the example of ERIC, an asbestos removal and abatement company. Around 1986, many US insurance companies faced a serious liability crisis due to asbestos claims. In response, they added an "absolute pollution exclusion" to their general commercial liability coverage. This left many client firms without any coverage for asbestos removal activities, underground storage tanks, hidden chemical problems, and so on. A small company, ERIC, decided to enter the very market from which everyone was retreating. ERIC believed that one could safely insure a building or warehouse if (1) an in-depth site analysis identified all major asbestos problems, (2) an insurance policy was tailored to the specific circumstance faced, and (3) subcontractors were trained and hired to perform any removal or abatement according to exacting standards. By combining engineering and actuarial analyses, plus having oversight control of subcontractors, an environmental insurance product was launched in segments that traditional insurers shunned. Reinsurers (such as Swiss Re) bought the concept, and ERIC has since sold millions of dollars of coverage.[46] In essence, ERIC reframed the problem to its advantage.

Phase 2: Intelligence Gathering

During the information-gathering phase, managers can succumb to various biases, including: (1) overconfidence, (2) flawed mental shortcuts, and (3) a bias toward confirming evidence. Overconfidence is a symptom of not knowing what we don't know. For example, 1,290 computer industry managers were asked a series of questions about their industry and asked to supply confidence ranges. In cases where they were 90% certain that the correct answer would be in their range, they were correct about only 20% of the time.[47]

Another set of biases stems from our mental shortcuts. For instance, when estimating next quarter's sales, a manager may follow the simple rule of basing it on last year's quarter. However, such convenient starting points often bias the final judgment because the manager gets overly anchored on that single number and does not adjust away from it enough. During periods of change, rules of thumb can become outdated quickly and even dangerously so. Alan Kantrow recounts a telling example from the infantry.[48] When a cannon was fired, two soldiers would stand at attention, one on the left and the other on the right, with one arm held up to chest height. No one knew the origin or purpose of this ritual. Upon investigation, they found that it traced back to the time that cannons were pulled on wagons by horses. The noise of the cannons firing frightened the horses, which needed to be held firmly. Although the horses vanished, the ritual of soldiers standing by remained. We can only wonder how many phantom horses still roam the corridors of today's organizations.

Bad judgment or choices may persist because of the third bias, a failure to search for disconfirming evidence. Managers seldom look for evidence that will disprove received wisdom. Organizational norms tend to reinforce this confirmation bias. Managers seek to affirm that the key assumptions underlying their actions are correct. It may take a new generation of managers or competing start-up companies to challenge the dominant logic of a firm or its industry and show that the impossible is achievable after all. In such cases, the performance organization—which needs to shield its core activities from disruption—is in deep conflict with the learning organization, which seeks to question, doubt, experiment, and break with the past. As George Santayana observed, most of us only believe what we see, "but we are much better at believing than at seeing."[49]

Phase 3: Coming to Conclusions

A deep-seated bias in the choice phase concerns people's dislike of uncertainty. This aversion inhibits innovation and exploration. People usually prefer a known risk to an unknown one, even if the latter has the same mathematical expectation.[50] For example, imagine that I ask you to draw a ball from one of two urns, each containing a mix of red and white balls. I promise you $100 if you draw a red ball and nothing if you draw a white. I tell you that urn 1 contains an even ratio of red to white balls and that urn 2 has an unknown ratio. Which urn would you select? Most people prefer urn 1, offering a known 50-50 chance of winning, even though urn 2 offers the same odds if you average out all possible ratios. And for those who don't believe urn 2 is a fair urn, they still prefer urn 1 if given the option to choose which color to bet on. We tend not to like situations with high ambiguity, whether it entails technological and market uncertainties or our strategy of making mistakes on purpose.

Other biases creep into the choice phase as well. People may deem intuitive choices to be better than they really are.[51] Or they assume that group decisions are necessarily better than individual choices, since two people know more than one. Although true in principle, groupthink and other dysfunctions are well-documented problems encountered in making team decisions.[52] In many organizations, decision making degenerates into a guessing game as to what senior management wants to hear. People abandon their better judgment in favor of what is politically correct, safe, or expedient. To counter this, leaders must encourage diversity of views and publicly challenge accepted wisdom. To be credible, they must also reward those who speak out and encourage deliberate mistakes.

Phase 4: Learning from Experience

In the final phase of the decision process, it is critical to pay full attention to the evolving feedback on the decision you just made. Such feedback is an important part of any learning process. Nevertheless, ego defenses, such as the tendency to rationalize bad outcomes, can distort this feedback, suppressing errors or obscuring important lessons. To counter this tendency, you must exercise the discipline of an athlete or a scientist, harnessing the hidden lessons contained in the real world's response to your actions. This means you need to be open to learning and traverse the top learning loops in figure 3-2 rather than the bottom ones, where denial, blame, and rationalization get in the way.[53]

One learning obstacle concerns the lack of sufficient feedback due to infrequent decisions, which makes it hard to separate signal and background noise. For example, how much can you learn from your decisions about renting an apartment or buying a car, since these occur relatively infrequently? It is hard to generalize from small samples and easy to overinterpret an isolated success or error. Another obstacle

Fig 3-2 Learning Loops

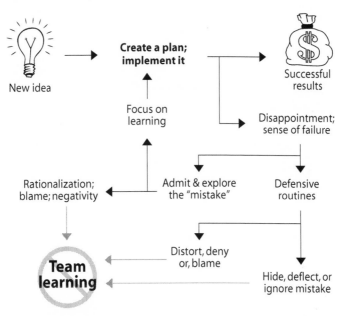

concerns missing feedback, such as not knowing what the option you rejected would have yielded. You will never know for sure how things would have worked out with the person you did not hire at work. A third obstacle to learning from experience concerns treatment effects, as in self-fulfilling prophecies. Teachers who hold favorable views of children when school starts will unconsciously influence them so that they do better than they might otherwise have done. This example was mentioned earlier and is known as the Pygmalion effect.[54]

When considering these and other obstacles, it becomes clear that true learning will require a scientific approach to control for confounding factors. As the quality control movement emphasizes the key is controlled variation. In some cases, fresh learning may require a separate organizational unit to fully block out indirect and unconscious influences from the old organizational culture. IBM adopted this path when developing its personal computer, as did General Motors for its Saturn project. To optimize efficient performance over the next few periods, a company should focus on what it knows best. However, to maximize its long-term survival chances, each company must occasionally challenge its core assumptions and extend its capabilities through experimentation. One resolution is that the main part of the organization focuses on short-term performance while a separate unit looks toward the long term. Ideally, however, the learning and performance cultures should interact. Otherwise, the learning organization may fail to leverage the organizational competencies that are at the core of the performing organization, or vice versa.

Better Decision Making

In real life, our decision processes are neither as linear nor as distinctly marked in time as figure 3-1 suggests. Information discovered in the intelligence-gathering stage may inspire you to go back and reframe your issue. Moreover, a complex problem, such as the relocation of your family or business, may entail a series of smaller decisions, each of which may involve several framing decisions, multiple intelligence-gathering efforts, and various coming-to-conclusions steps.

In spite of this complexity, it helps to think about each of the stages of a decision separately. Avoiding error is easier once you can recognize the stages and know the most common traps. You can't guard against the characteristic errors of each stage unless you recognize which part of the decision you're working on. Importantly, we should not just learn from our own mistakes but especially those of others. To paraphrase Santayana's famous observation about history, those who don't study other people's mistakes are doomed to repeat them.

Since there are so many ways in which we can err, here are some basic tips for better decision making from the perspective of making productive mistakes:

1. Uncover the implicit assumptions underlying any important decision and then challenge them with the help of others. Find an easy way to test some key assumptions.
2. Look at important decisions through the eyes of the performance and learning cultures. The latter will make you more accepting of experimental approaches.
3. Realize that estimates may be overconfident or anchored on readily available numbers. Be honest about what you don't know; see if a smart mistake can make you wiser.
4. Look at confirming, but especially at disconfirming, evidence. Try to disprove key assumptions underlying the firm's dominant logic and use this to recalibrate risk.
5. Balance the risks of "shooting from the hip" with "analysis paralysis." Consider intuition a valid decision input, but don't trust it blindly unless you are very experienced.
6. Don't assume that groups always make better decisions; unless you manage the group process well, the team IQ may be lower than the group average (that is, groupthink may be operating).
7. Experience is automatic; learning is not. Even if you have good feedback, the implicit lessons may not be evident at first. Try to correct for distortion and missing data.
8. Balance a learning culture with that of the performance organization. If you are in a leadership role, accept some degree of failure as a necessary price of learning.
9. Adopt a humble view about how much we know about the complex, changing world around us. Try often to challenge and test potentially outdated assumptions.

This chapter showed that there are many ways to err and examined some of the underlying reasons, which can range from poor framing to repeating the same error twice. Whatever the reasons, each mistake presents you with an opportunity to see what it can teach you about the world at large. Any mismatch between what you expected to happen and what actually happens presents a valuable learning moment, in principle. But to extract the lessons, you need an attitude and a mind-set oriented toward learning. This means overcoming our natural tendencies to deny, suppress, distort, and forget about mistakes. Also, you need a conceptual framework for diagnosing your mistake, such as the four-phase framework I presented. Lastly, if you accept that mistakes are valuable and that making a few more might be a good strategy at times, you need a road map for deciding when and where to err. This brings us to the second part of the book: making mistakes on purpose.

Part Two
Designing for Mistakes

CHAPTER 4

Faster Learning
A Practical Road Map

Experience is the name we give to our mistakes.
—OSCAR WILDE[55]

In this chapter, I encourage you to make more, better, faster mistakes, all in the spirit of accelerating your learning. I propose models and examples from worlds as divergent as venture capital and dating, and show you how the principles applied by bold entrepreneurs and successful serial dates can pay dividends in other areas. I then introduce some principles from the philosophy of science, such as disconfirmation strategies. My aim, overall, is to teach you a strategic approach to mistakes.

This chapter is also a practical how-to guide. Using an actual business case, I introduce a three-stage screening process that demonstrates how useful it can be to purposefully violate particular assumptions. This is a concrete methodology rooted in psychological as well as decision theoretic principles. It will help you sort through the numerous beliefs you hold dear and identify those most worthy of testing. Throughout, I will help you recognize the manner in which intuition and meta-strategies, as well as optimization models, can help you to accelerate your learning via purposeful mistakes.

Entrepreneurs: Expert Mistake Makers

A successful entrepreneur was interviewed by a reporter about his many accomplishments. The interchange went as follows:

Reporter:	Sir, what was the key to your success?
Entrepreneur:	Good decisions.
Reporter:	And what was the key to those good decisions?
Entrepreneur:	Experience.
Reporter:	And where, sir, did that experience come from?
Entrepreneur:	Bad decisions.

Most entrepreneurs, and the venture capitalists who invest in them, live by a bold mantra: fail fast, often, and cheaply. Just like Thomas Edison and Sir James Dyson, inventors we looked at in chapter 2, you should view multiple errors as the path to success. Remember that early-stage inventors, like entrepreneurs, usually don't even use the term *mistakes* for these early and necessary missteps, preferring "experiments," "protocols," or "tests" instead. Google's IPO prospectus, a serious financial document for investors heavily vetted by lawyers, contains a startling statement: "We would fund projects that have a 10% chance of earning a billion dollars. . . . Do not be surprised if we place smaller bets in areas that seem very speculative or even strange." Google is warning investors not to be taken aback if the company takes actions that may seem odd or wrong. The art of making mistakes is to separate costly, foolish mistakes that teach you little from those clever, cheap mistakes that can offer you the world.

The question then becomes, what qualities must entrepreneurs have to succeed—other than, of course, a high tolerance for risk? Surely even the boldest venture capital firm does not select at random. What criteria do they apply for upping the ante of mistakes that will lead to brilliant insights (and payoffs)?

Jesse Treu is a senior partner with Domain Associates, a venture capital firm based in Princeton, New Jersey, specializing in pharmaceuticals, devices, and diagnostics. Domain has been very successful over many decades. When Treu, who has a PhD in physics from Princeton University, examined Domain's past successes and failures, he noticed that most of the successful ventures had changed their business plan and even their business model. The unsuccessful ones, in contrast, were hesitant to change their plans. Instead, according to Treu, they remained stuck with the wrong strategy for too long, hampering their chances of success.[56] This finding might seem counterintuitive: remember the mantra "stick to your knitting"? Nevertheless, it highlights an important truism. In the venture capital game, leaders and management teams who know how to adapt are far more valuable than the best-laid plans.

As Prussian general Helmuth von Moltke observed, "No plan survives contact with the enemy."[57] The same is true in business: few plans survive contact with reality. The key in entrepreneurship and innovation is to speed up the learning process and separate false beliefs from sound ones at a faster pace. This leaves us with the need for broad strategies that guide us with such questions as: How many mistakes should we make in a given year, and of which kind? What is and should be our personal or organizational tolerance for mistakes? Are we really ready and willing to make deliberate mistakes to learn faster? How should we follow the advice of IBM founder Thomas J. Watson Sr., who famously said, "If you want to succeed faster, make more mistakes"?[58]

To Err Can Be Divine

Let's start with a task most of us have personal experience with: the dating game. Most dating is tremendously inefficient. People can go on many, many dates, enduring countless glasses of wine and hours of late-night talks, before they locate that compatible someone—if they ever do! Tried-and-true approaches include traditional networking, introductions via family and friends, and even arranged marriage. In recent years, social media networking and techniques like speed dating and matchmaking websites, with their near-endless multiplicity of available partners, have provided alternative vistas, allowing those searching for love to experience a higher degree of "deal flow" (to borrow a term from venture capital). The benefit of these new approaches, of course, is that they allow you to filter quickly and save time; the risk is that the wide net of options and pressure to decide quickly cause you to throw out the baby with the bathwater.

Maria Dahvana Headley, a 20-year-old New York University drama student, took a daring approach. After many fruitless forays into the New York City dating scene, she decided to try a bold and outrageous experiment: letting go of her selection criteria. She resolved to say yes to anyone who asked her out on a date (with the exception of murderers and rapists). As she writes in her memoir, *The Year of Yes*, this policy led to dates with her building's maintenance head, a homeless man, a Microsoft millionaire who still lived with his mother, and a career woman.[59] She finally accepted a date with a divorced playwright. Although she would not have given him a second chance before the experiment—he was many years her senior and had children from a previous relationship— she fell in love and is now happily married. By permitting many mistakes in dating, Headley was able to learn faster about what she truly wanted in a partner. She then found her special partner more quickly. Headley's epiphany was that our typical way of experimenting—developing a preconceived idea of Mr. or Ms. Right and finding someone to fit the part—does not always lead to the best decisions. Making more mistakes, as Headley did in her year of saying yes, can speed the process of learning.

If we were perfectly rational, we would have no need to make mistakes or engage in random behaviors in order to learn. But human beings are far from rational, and therefore need to allow random error into their lives in order to succeed. As Francis Bacon wrote, "A wise man will make more opportunities than he finds."[60] Deliberately creating portals of discovery requires being open to experiments and mistakes.

From the standpoint of cognitive psychology, here is why we need to make mistakes on purpose—why doing so can help us transcend our own bounded rationality:

- **We are overconfident.** Most of us are blind to the limits of what we know and don't know, a bias researchers call overconfidence.[61] Paradoxically, as research has shown, expertise does not always protect us; sometimes it can hamper our ability to learn. Inexperienced managers make many mistakes and often learn from them. Experienced managers may become so good at the game they're used to playing that they can no longer see ways to improve significantly. If you have reached a plateau, you may need to make deliberate mistakes to shake yourself out of your narrow comfort zones and elevate your game to higher levels.

- **We are risk-averse.** Our professional and personal pride is tied up in being right. Even if we exhibit humility in private about our knowledge and insight, we are very reluctant to submit our fragile egos to explicit tests that might show we have been wrong all along. Employees are rewarded for producing good results and penalized for failures, so they spend a great deal of time and energy trying not to make mistakes. Furthermore, people register losses with more feeling than gains. That's why few would flip a fair coin for $1,000. Since losses loom larger psychologically than gains, people tend to be risk-averse and fail to experiment as much as they might. This bias is compounded by people looking at risk in isolation rather than through a portfolio lens, in which diversification and the law of averages get their full due. We shall examine this bias further in chapter 6.

- **We seek confirming evidence.** Because we tend to favor data that support our beliefs, we often don't see the alternatives or ask contrarian questions. We want to be right, not wrong. In classic studies on experimenter bias, Robert Rosenthal showed that students conducting maze learning experiments with rats produced results that confirmed their prior expectations.[62] Some students thought they had been given smart rats and others thought they had been given dumb rats; this assumption was based on the label they saw on two boxes from which the rats were taken. In fact, they were all similar rats who had been placed at random in the two boxes ahead of time, before the class convened. Nonetheless, when Rosenthal reviewed the results, the students who thought they had smart rats reported faster mazing learning time than the other group.

- **We assume feedback is reliable.** Few environments offer reliable enough feedback to extract clear lessons immediately. Mostly, managers function in "wicked" environments where feedback is lacking or misleading.[63] Consider again the maze learning experiment with rats just mentioned. The researchers thought the experiment would be quite objective since the students were given clear instructions about how to run the maze learning trials and would be graded on their lab reports. However, unconsciously, the students introduced errors when recording and interpreting the data. When writing down the time it took for their rat to find the cheese in the maze, they might round the clock measurement upward or downward in line with their expectation. Or when later writing their report, they might confuse a sloppily handwritten "3" for an "8." In the real world, the learning environment will be even more challenging, due to measurement error, missing data, random noise, and confounding influences that skew the results. As a result, many of the things we believe may simply not be true.

Disconfirming Evidence

Philosophers of science have argued that falsification is the fastest way to the truth.[64] Falsification entails trying to disprove your hypotheses and when they prove wrong, testing new ones. Similarly, making mistakes can be the quickest way to discover a problem's solution. Using a classic decision-making problem, I ask managers to find the underlying pattern in a sequence of three numbers, such as 2, 4, 6. The participants are allowed to propose alternative sets of three numbers and will be told whether they fit the pattern.[65] Most people formulate a preliminary hypothesis—in the case of 2, 4, 6, they might guess that the pattern is even, ascending, sequential numbers. Of course, other hypotheses are plausible, such as the last number being the sum of the previous two or the last number being three times the first number, and so on. Forming some kind of hypothesis is generally a good idea, especially if there are many hypotheses than can be empirically tested, as in this example. But an insidious confirmation bias may creep in when people actually devise strategies to test their hypothesis. Should they test a set of numbers that fits their initial guess or one that violates it? Most people gravitate toward testing sequences that fit their rule, as illustrated in the "Testing a Hypothesis" column of the table (which includes the yes-or-no answers to whether each test sequence fits the hidden pattern underlying 2, 4, 6).

	A. Testing a Hypothesis (for example, even, ascending sequential numbers)	Does the guess fit the presumed pattern?	B. Making Deliberate Decisions (testing the opposite)	Does the guess fit the presumed pattern?
Initial sequence	2, 4, 6		2, 4, 6	
Test 1	4, 6, 8	Yes	4, 6, 11	Yes
Test 2	10, 12, 14	Yes	5, 2, 1	No
Test 3	126, 128, 130	Yes	-10, 0, 546	Yes
Guess of pattern	*Even*, sequential, ascending numbers		*Any* ascending numbers	
Result	*Wrong answer*		*Right answer*	

After three successful tests, participants usually state with great confidence that the "even, ascending, sequential numbers" hypothesis is correct. But they are wrong.

Consider the alternative approach of testing sequences that violate the hypothesis (shown in the fourth column)—in other words, making deliberate mistakes. Participants who choose numbers that don't fit their current hypothesis are usually faster to discover that the real pattern is *any* ascending sequence. The pattern is rarely uncovered unless subjects are willing to make mistakes—that is, to test numbers that violate their belief. Instead, most people get stuck in a narrow and wrong hypothesis, as often happens in real life, such that their only way out is to make a mistake that turns out not to be a mistake after all.

Sometimes, committing errors is not just the fastest way to the correct answer, it's the only way. College students presented with this experiment were allowed to test as many sets of three numbers as they wished. Fewer than 10% discovered the pattern. The vast majority became locked into a narrow hypothesis, such as even sequential numbers, and they tested only combinations of numbers that would fit that pattern. In the short run, they were correct to use this approach. But in the long run, they were wrong, because they didn't experiment widely enough to discover the underlying pattern.[66] Whenever you have little hard evidence to go on, the chances are low that you'll be correct in your initial guess about how the pieces fit together. The fastest way to find the pattern is to try many disconfirming tests.

Disciplined, Deliberate Mistake-Making

There is, of course, no shortage of mistakes to be made. How, then, do you distinguish smart ones from foolish ones? In some cases, it's obvious: no wise person would jump from a bridge just to see if it was dangerous to fall. But most real-life scenarios aren't so black and white. For example: should you hire a person you think won't work out to test your core assumptions about what it takes to succeed in your organization? Should you send your team down a path you aren't sure will yield results, just for the benefit of broadening your collective wisdom?

At the management consulting firm I founded, Decision Strategies International (DSI), I decided to implement a disciplined process of deliberate mistake-making. I used a five-step process to identify and then execute a few "smart" mistakes—tests that we were willing to pursue in full knowledge that they would probably fail. My colleagues and I were willing to challenge our thinking because we sought to obtain new insights about how to run our business. Also, we committed collectively to making sure that the cost of failure of any mistakes we made would be manageable.

I convened the management team of our company and asked them to identify key assumptions underlying our approach to running the business. We then scored the assumptions to see which would be the best candidates for testing in the spirit of a deliberate mistake. I describe the process we followed and some of the conclusions we drew— which led us to alter how we approach our business:

Step 1. Identify assumptions. DSI's leaders began by identifying the most cherished assumptions we have about how best to run our consulting business. In so doing, we generated the raw material with which to make mistakes that might reveal flaws in our reasoning. The following are ten of the assumptions we identified:

1. Cold-calling on Fortune 100 clients will not work; we need a senior champion in the client organization.
2. Our clients buy primarily on trust and reputation, with limited price sensitivity; they don't send out a request for proposal (RFP).
3. Young MBAs don't work well for us; we need experienced consultants on the team.
4. Bundled pricing is better than pricing each project's components separately.
5. Senior partners must get more pay from their billing bonus than from their base salary.
6. Formal interviews with clients must always be done by two consultants, with one taking notes.
7. The firm can be successfully run by a president who is not a major billing senior consultant.
8. Executive education and consulting are natural cross-selling activities.

9. Books and articles are key to our firm's image as cutting-edge and rigorous.
10. It is not worthwhile to respond to RFPs, since clients who use them are usually price shopping or looking for options to reject a choice already made.

Because a company's leadership may not be aware of all of the assumptions it makes, executives should ask colleagues throughout the organization to help construct the list. For example, in addition to senior executives you can ask the head of IT or even a trusted partner or loyal customer. The key is to focus on assumptions that lie at the core of the business in such areas as strategy, operations, marketing, finance, legal, IT, human resources, and so on.

Step 2. Select assumptions for testing. The management team then ranked the ten assumptions by two metrics: (1) significance to how we ran the business and (2) confidence in the accuracy or correctness of the assumption. To assess importance, we asked what we would do differently if we knew that a given assumption was false. The greater the impact on the organization of discovering that the assumption was false, the higher it would be scored in terms of importance. To assess accuracy, we asked how much we would be willing to bet that the assumption was correct (would we bet the company or our lives?). Figure 4-1 shows how the ten assumptions were actually plotted on our two scoring dimensions.

We then honed in on those assumptions that scored high on importance and less high on certainty in their correctness. This left us with assumptions 3, 7, and 10.

Step 3. Rank the assumptions. For the three assumptions thus identified, we asked company managers the five questions shown in table 4-1. The intent was to generate an overall

Fig 4-1 Score and Map Key Assumptions

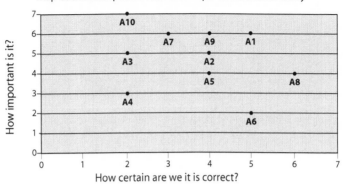

Map each assumption in terms of importance and certainty

score indicating the relative value of putting these assumptions to the test. To keep things simple, we gave each question equal weight. Based on this scoring process, assumption 10, which related to our company's view about RFPs, was identified as having the highest potential of benefiting from a strategy of deliberate mistakes.

Table 4-1 Rank the Assumptions

How true is the following? *(scale 1=not true; 7=very true)*	**A3**	**A7**	**A10**
1. Potential benefit of experiment relative to its cost is high	5	6	6
2. We make this decision repeatedly	4	2	5
3. This is a complex problem to solve analytically	6	3	4
4. Our experience base with this assumption is limited	4	3	5
5. The business conditions surrounding this issue have changed	2	4	6
	21	18	26

Step 4. Create strategies for making mistakes. Instead of never responding to RFPs, which was the firm's policy, it was decided to act in earnest on the next RFP. This meant making the "mistake" of responding to an RFP that came over the transom. As it happened, we'd recently received an RFP from a regional electric utility. To keep our costs down, management assigned recent hires to develop an initial proposal, both to help them learn how to structure engagements and also to limit time spent on this by our senior partners. But the RFP was taken seriously and developed with customary care.

Step 5. Execute the mistake. Our firm produced a customized response to the RFP, listing the partners' normal fees, resulting in a budget of about $200,000 for this relatively small consulting project. To our surprise, the electric utility invited our firm to visit with the CEO and the senior management team to explore not only the project in question but others as well. After learning more about our firm's capabilities, the electric utility signed a separate project on short notice before awarding the original proposal. Additional work followed, amounting to more than $1 million of additional consulting in the pipeline from this client. Not a bad return for making a small mistake.

Step 6. Learn from the process. Mistakes cost time and money. Whether the mistake is a success or a failure, conduct a careful analysis after the exercise to understand what you have learned. How does the result reinforce or change your assumptions? What were the surprises? How might the results change your business? What other experiments or mistakes might be useful based on this experience? The key is to recognize that any surprising result, whether due to an action you took or did not take, is a learning opportunity. Whenever your expectation diverges from reality, you should try to figure out why.

The relatively low-cost deliberate mistake made by our firm has changed our thinking about RFPs and about mistake-making in general. We look at new RFPs in a different way and have responded to several that we would have ignored in the past. DSI is also, as a result of this experiment, testing some other cherished assumptions that surfaced, including the other two assumptions listed in table 4-1 (numbers 3 and 7). Hiring young MBAs (to test 3) is obviously easier than changing the CEO running the firm (to test 7), so the firm has hired some junior staff. And we are experimenting with a shift in the president's balance between consulting and management as a low-cost approach to test assumption 7.

Performance versus Learning

While you can often learn faster by making more mistakes, it's also fair to acknowledge that learning is *not* always the most important goal. There are critical moments, and specifics tasks, where high performance should and will be your only concern. If you have your hands on the stick of a Boeing 747 airplane at 30,000 feet in the air, or if you are elbow-deep in a patient's chest during open heart surgery—please, do not think about making mistakes! Focus on counting your surgical instruments and making sure it all returns to the table before you close up the patient. Make sure you perform the brain surgery on the correct side of the head and on the right patient. We'll all thank you for *not* being focused on learning!

But when the surgery is over, when the plane is on the ground, perhaps it *will* make sense for you to reflect on what you've learned and explore ways to make deliberate mistakes. If you are a pilot, perhaps you can step into the flight simulator and try crashing the virtual plane in all kinds of challenging circumstances, from hurricane weather conditions to failing engines or land-based rocket attacks. You will be a better pilot for it. As passengers, we will be glad you did. When you walk out of the operating room, it might not be a bad idea to do simulations to prepare you for unusually complex challenges you could face or to try out new surgical procedures on human cadavers or animals.

Mistakes are often painful and embarrassing. We hate to lose. In Japan, some executives still commit seppuku, a ritualized suicide, when they fail. We often tend to deny our mistakes rather than learning from them. Few of us, deep down, want to make more mistakes. So we face a conundrum: we dislike mistakes, yet this is often the only way to get ahead. This book shines a different light upon mistakes by helping you to understand what they are and how they can help you make better decisions in the future. If we know how to use them, mistakes create opportunities. They can be vital portals to discovery. Also, make sure to take a look at the mistakes of your colleagues and see what you can learn from them. The biggest error we can make is not to fully appreciate the power of mistakes to change our approach to business and life in general.

CHAPTER 5

Deliberate Mistakes
Creating Portals of Discovery

So go ahead and make mistakes. Make all you can. Because that's where you will find success. On the far side of failure.
—THOMAS J. WATSON SR., FOUNDER OF IBM[67]

Throughout this chapter, we'll continue to explore the counterintuitive notion of making mistakes on purpose to challenge deeply held views that are perhaps wrong. I also discuss when making deliberate mistakes can be of greatest value, recognizing that many of them will likely be blind alleys.

In general, there are two kinds of approaches to purposeful mistake-making. The first one is to defy conventional wisdom and instead follow your own intuition (as in the classic case of the Wright brothers learning to fly). The second approach is to act at cross-purposes to your *own* views, with the aim of challenging (and thereby, potentially, strengthening and expanding) your own mental framework. Advertising genius David Ogilvy did this when running advertisements he thought would *not* work, to see if his thinking about marketing was still fresh. Many of these ads failed, but some succeeded—such as the famous Hathaway man with the eye patch—giving Ogilvy a continual edge.[68]

Making Mistakes on Purpose

Imagine yourself as the head of a company that manufactures pet food. You monitor your sales chiefly through supermarkets, which are your main point of distribution. Suppose that some young recent hire comes to you and argues that your business is actually in *decline*, even though your recent data clearly demonstrate a steady hold on market share. This young employee recommends that the company start monitoring nontraditional channels, like pet superstores and direct sales through veterinarians. To get this new data would add considerable cost and reduce profits. Your analytical mind compels you to conduct a preliminary cost-benefit trade-off. This analysis suggests that you would be wasting marketing budget and might look foolish. But your intuition tells you that the young employee might be onto something, although you can't put your finger on what it is. Would you go with your hunch or let the spreadsheet do the talking?

This scenario represents a real business case. As it turned out, the pet food manufacturer *did* invest in the new monitoring, just as the young employee suggested. This new channel data enabled them to see that their market share *was* indeed in decline. Adhering to their tried-and-true method of relying on supermarket sales was placing the company at serious risk of obsolescence. Consumers were increasingly purchasing pet food through alternative channels, and the company was missing these growth opportunities. Senior management was able to get ahead of this unrecognized fall in market share, realign its sales and distribution strategy, and start to monitor trends in customer behavior more carefully.

A decision that seemed, from a traditional perspective, like a mistake—investing in new monitoring systems, even though this didn't seem justified in terms of cost—turned out to be opportune for this company. Deliberate mistakes can have great value in environments of rapid change, complexity, and chaos. And if the assumptions tested involve repeated decision making, the benefits of new insights can be multiplied many times over. In these kinds of environments there is a high opportunity of garnering new, brilliant insights, changing the game, and harnessing significant benefits. In situations where decisions are routine and mostly standardized, such as banks reviewing consumer loans, new insights that allow even a marginal advantage have the potential for enormous cumulative benefits. I demonstrate this next in an actual case about the US Bell System and then broaden the lens to explore deeper questions behind purposeful mistake-making. Finally, I present conditions that favor deliberate mistakes. The chapter concludes with personal and organizational obstacles that might stand in the way of exploring new venues widely.

Challenging the Existing Model

Prior to the breakup of the Bell System in 1984, US telephone companies were required to offer service to every household in their region, regardless of each consumer's credit history. Throughout the United States, there were approximately 12 million new subscribers each year, with bad debts in excess of $450 million. As protection against both credit risk and loss of their equipment, the law permitted each company to demand a security deposit from a small percentage of new subscribers. Each Bell operating company had developed its own statistical model to determine which customers posed the greatest risk and charged those customers the deposit. Most companies presumed, naturally, that poor credit equaled high risk, but it was hard for them to put this important presumption to the test. The companies asked the geniuses in their famous Bell Labs for some advice. These scientists, many of whom had deep training in statistics and quantitative modeling, came back with some rather counterintuitive advice: they suggested *suspending* the policy of levying the high-risk customers with deposits in order to see what would happen. To senior management, this advice seemed like a frightening, potentially damaging proposition: a high-stakes, deliberate mistake.

Nevertheless, the Bell Labs scientists defended the logic of their position. Behind Bell's existing policy was a tacit assumption: people with bad credit were more likely to abuse equipment or fail to pay their phone bills. The Bell Labs scientists were not willing to accept that as de facto truth. They argued that only a carefully controlled experiment could reveal how those asked for deposits might behave when no security deposit was paid. The scientists wanted an evidence-based point of view of how customers with poor credit behaved in comparison with the rest of the population. Management acquiesced, and the experiment began. For a period of several months, new subscribers were not asked for a security deposit. To the surprise of many, quite a few of the presumed "bad" customers paid their bills fully and on time. The likelihood of theft and damage to phones and related equipment was lower than it was among several segments of the "good" customers. Clearly, the current risk models were missing some key predictors.

Armed with these new insights, Bell Labs was able to use the full data set to get a better picture of the behavior of new subscribers. Multiple regression analysis then allowed them to set up better prediction models. For example, the weight to give to repayment record, discretionary income, type of employment, years at residence, and other risk factors could be changed. The operating companies recalibrated their credit scoring models accordingly and started to use far more effective screening strategies. The improved credit models added an average of $137 million to the bottom line every year for a decade.

In this situation—where repetitive, standardized decisions were required—a deliberate mistake yielded valuable insight. The repeat application of the new, more accurate scoring models for identifying deposit customers were applied day after day, year after year—leading to a very high payoff. Eventually, it became clear that the long-term benefits of the new strategy clearly outweighed the initial, up-front cost of suspending the original deposit policy. However, this was not evident to the company's leaders at the time that the decision was made. These insights, and the payoff, could only emerge after the leaders purposely acted in ways that looked, at first glance, ill-advised.

The Paradox of Deliberate Mistakes

The phrase "deliberate mistake" contains an element of paradox that may not sit well with more exacting readers. Is a deliberate mistake *truly* an error—or is it, by definition, a purposeful act of testing or experimentation?

The answer to this question depends on how you view the human mind. In the classic economic definition of human thought, the human mind is *unitary*. It is presumed that an individual operates from a single, consistent mind-set, with beliefs and values all in alignment. Traditional economics is built on this rationality assumption. It is assumed that each individual has clearly articulated, consistent preferences (measured via utility functions) and also that each person holds coherent beliefs (measured via subjective probabilities). This hyper-rational view of humans can be a useful fiction, especially as a first-order approximation in traditional economic models, but it's not what I assume here.

Instead, I ask you to view the human mind as operating at multiple levels at once, with alternative and sometimes even competing points of view. Imagine this as multiple persons residing within a single mind. And, no, don't worry—I'm not talking about the Freudian struggle between the id and the superego or invoking the notion of multiple personalities. I am simply referring to the way in which a person can be of two minds about a complex issue. This more nuanced view of thinking has been common in psychology and is increasingly gaining traction in economics as well, as the fields of behavioral finance and economics continue to grow. Since this view underlies my case for the strategy of purposeful mistakes, let's examine it in some more depth.

The human mind contains multiple layers of functioning, but for the sake of simplicity, let's start with just two. Cognitive psychologists refer to the two primary functions of our minds as System 1 and System 2. These two systems correspond to what some call "right and left brain" and others call "intuition versus analytical reasoning." But since these terms carry long legacies and tend to drag in other preconceived notions, cognitive psychologists prefer the neutrality and clinical detachment of their labels. Here is how the 2002 Nobel laureate in economics, Professor Daniel Kahneman, a leading cognitive researcher, explains the distinction. System 1 thinking is the most common and comprises "thoughts that come to mind on their own." As Kahneman describes it, "It's not like we're on automatic pilot, but we respond to the world in ways that we're not conscious of, that we don't control." When operating in System 1 mode, our thoughts are "fast, effortless, associative, and often emotionally charged; they're also governed by habit, so they're difficult either to modify or to control."

For illustration's sake here, let's think of System 1 thought as a person, and let's call that person Jessie. Jessie is impulsive and emotional, maybe a little unpredictable, and usually operates from intuition or gut instinct rather than long deliberation. System 2 thought, in contrast, is our reason-driven mode. As described by Kahneman: "System 2 is . . . conscious, it's deliberate; it's slower, serial, effortful, and deliberately controlled, but it can follow rules."[69] Again, just for our purposes here, let's imagine a person named Max as System 2. Max is disciplined and rule-abiding. Max loves structure and never acts without conscious deliberation.

Implicit in this more complex view of the brain is that no one person is purely Jessie or Max. We all have a bit of Jessie and Max in us. This is why we have competing instincts and modes of being within our mind. Different situations will draw one or the other into dominance. Whether or not an action is determined as a mistake depends on the mode of thinking that is currently dominant. Jessie, for example, might feel it's a waste of time to go to a just-released movie, but Max might be able to justify the same decision as an experiment. It would be a deliberate mistake for Jessie to go see the movie, since this would go against an initial instinct and dominant decision mode. Conversely, it's easy to imagine that Max, facing a decision like choosing a new hire from 10 interview candidates, would use a spreadsheet and rank each person according to a set of criteria. But suppose that Max decides not to go with the highest scoring candidate, because of an intuition that the third-ranked person is actually better. This would be a deliberate mistake for Max, since he would go against his preferred mode of choosing.

It is this tension between System 1 and System 2, between the Jessie and the Max in each of us, that creates the sense of paradox when we use the phrase "deliberate mistake." To circle back to our original question: whether or not a given action is a deliberate mistake depends on whether that action goes against the grain of our dominant decision style in the given situation. Since humans use both systems—since we are all Max *and* Jessie, in different blends—any one person's dominant style can differ by type of problem and occasion. You might be analytical when buying a car but impulse-driven when you decide who to marry. You might behave like Max, coolheaded and data-driven, when arguing with your colleagues, but apply a Jessie style, all hotheaded emotion, when debating with your spouse. For those trying to balance these cognitive modes in any one decision, there will be a kind of System 3 level of thinking.[70] This gets us into the complex research domain of inner conflict resolution, personality theory, cognitive style, and decision modeling. But we don't need all this refinement for my definition of a deliberate mistake. It simply is an action we take that runs counter to whichever system is normally driving the decision, which could be System 1, 2, or 3.

Practical Applications

Generally, mistakes should be encouraged whenever long-term learning is more important to you than short-term performance. Consider the strategy of deliberate mistakes as one of many tools that managers can employ when operating on the right side of the knowledge spectrum, as depicted in figure 5-1.

Fig 5-1 Navigating the Knowledge Spectrum

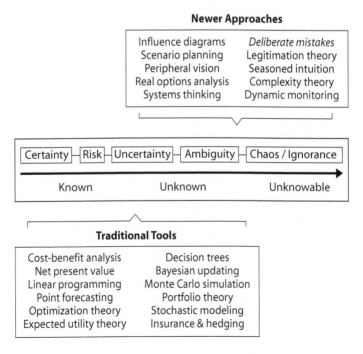

Newer Approaches

Influence diagrams	*Deliberate mistakes*
Scenario planning	Legitimation theory
Peripheral vision	Seasoned intuition
Real options analysis	Complexity theory
Systems thinking	Dynamic monitoring

Certainty — Risk — Uncertainty — Ambiguity — Chaos / Ignorance

Known	Unknown	Unknowable

Traditional Tools

Cost-benefit analysis	Decision trees
Net present value	Bayesian updating
Linear programming	Monte Carlo simulation
Point forecasting	Portfolio theory
Optimization theory	Stochastic modeling
Expected utility theory	Insurance & hedging

This figure depicts a spectrum of knowledge, ranging from that which we can be certain about to that which is out of our grasp. Some decisions, such as what to order for lunch or where a company like McDonald's should choose to locate its next building, are on the left side of the spectrum. Presumably you know what you like to eat and what's available at the deli downstairs. Likewise, McDonald's has already built around 20,000 restaurants worldwide and has reams of data and experience to support any choice. So these types of decisions are grounded in highly familiar terrain, and the decision tools employed here should be the tried-and-true ones. They include forecasting techniques, net present value (NPV) analysis, and various optimization methods. For example, banks deciding on routine credit applications can effectively use statistical models, risk analysis, and computer simulation to optimize their loan portfolio.

But often we encounter decisions that throw us into unfamiliar terrain, like entering an unknown market, launching a new product, or developing an emerging technology. These decisions move you onto shaky ground—the far right side of the knowledge spectrum, where uncertainty and ambiguity, or even ignorance and chaos, reign. The right side of this spectrum is where Jessie, our intuitive System 1 thinker, is most at home and where Max, our System 2 thinker, feels like a fish out of water. The right side of the knowledge spectrum is where inventors live, at the boundary of knowledge. Entrepreneurs labor there as well, since they must continually fine-tune their business model or reshape the organization. In these circumstances, good data and strong analytical tools can't help you much. Instead, you need tools that will let you learn faster and manage a dynamic, fluid situation. This is where scenario planning, systems thinking, and deliberate mistake-making can help.[71]

There are, of course, circumstances in which the strategy of deliberate mistakes is too costly. Imagine an oil company that drills speculatively in new locations. Even by using the best decision models available, it expects that 9 of 10 wells it drills will be dry. There are high costs associated with each new drilling. Should this oil company deliberately drill holes in locations it assumes have little chance of success, just to test its deepest assumptions about drilling? Likely not—such a mistake would seem unwise. In situations like this, where mistakes come at high cost, you need to be judicious about the trade-off between the cost of acting in error and the potential benefits of learning. This is especially difficult if you don't know the limitations of your knowledge base (how far you are off the mark), and even more challenging if you don't know what you don't know. Some might argue that even in the drilling example here, it might pay to challenge *some* key assumptions, like the software you depend on for selecting your location or the manner in which you construct teams to collaborate on the ground. Such "tests," however, would be best approached piecemeal—through small, low-risk steps rather than through a single, multi-million–dollar bet. This approach is known as real options thinking and comes close to what I recommend here.[72] But real options still meet the test of offering a positive expected value or utility, whereas deliberate mistakes—as defined in this book—fail to meet that test.

Conditions That Favor Deliberate Mistakes

Considering the cost of deliberate mistakes and the high probability of failure, you need to be strategic about when to pursue them. Generally speaking, the strategy of committing mistakes on purpose is most effective when some of the following conditions hold true:

- **There is much to gain relative to the cost of the mistake.** In the oil company example, the high cost of each speculative drilling means that the likelihood of a payoff for an experiment would need to be very high to justify a potential mistake. By contrast, in the Bell System example, the enormity of the potential payoff (a reduction of $450 million of total bad debt) made it far more opportune to take risks that could lead to new insights. In general, the cost of a deliberate mistake that fails (one that turns out to have no value) should be considered relative to the potential rewards (including learning) if it succeeds. Naturally, companies need to limit risks in their mistake-making and avoid mistakes that could be catastrophic. Testing experimental equipment that you expect to fail in a jet filled with passengers would be highly irresponsible; testing it in a simulator would be smart because the cost of failure is reduced.

- **Decisions are made repeatedly.** When core assumptions drive frequently made decisions, such as those about hiring, running ads, assessing credit risks, or making promotion decisions, a strategy of making deliberate mistakes is likely to be valuable. When Citibank first proposed extending credit card offers to college students, many considered this idea to be a big mistake. According to conventional wisdom, students were terrible credit risks—immature youngsters with no job or home, high debts, and limited or no credit history.

    Though it was clearly a mistake by traditional standards, Citibank reaped high rewards, both in terms of an increased customer base (many of these students evolved into valuable long-term customers) and insights derived from the experiment (many parents, it turns out, will bail out student cardholders when they run into the red). Again, as with the Bell decisions about whether or not a deposit should be levied, Citibank's new business offering relied on repeated, frequent, standardized decisions. For rare or onetime decisions, such as a company's choice of whether to relocate its headquarters or engage in a merger, deliberate mistakes make little sense. In those cases, it is better to rely on received wisdom, test core assumptions in the margin, and learn from the mistakes of others.

- **The environment is in flux.** Whenever the world changes, people and organizations need to make mistakes to fully appreciate how the new reality affects their mode of operating. In these situations, mistakes are often unavoidable and inadvertent, because current approaches are no longer effective. But making deliberate mistakes on top of the inadvertent ones can help you accelerate learning.

  Procter & Gamble, for example, operates in the fickle consumer product market, where very few product introductions succeed. Their policy is: fail often, fast, and cheap. When they discovered that their old product development models were becoming less effective, P&G challenged their long-held assumption that in-house innovations would be most successful and turned to outside partners for new products. One result of this new "connect and develop" strategy was the highly successful SpinBrush.[73] In a changing environment, the strategic advantage shifts to those who learn fastest, and this may require deliberate mistakes.

- **The problem is complex and solutions numerous.** The more complex an environment becomes, the more likely it will be that your understanding of the situation is incomplete. Making deliberate mistakes can help expose flaws in your mental models and reveal other ways of approaching a problem. In the entertainment business, the rise of cable, the Internet, TiVo, and the i-devices (such as the iPod, iPad, and iPhone) has created a complex, multi-variable environment. Experiments and mistakes are of paramount importance. Some of the most successful entertainment innovations, from 24-hour news channels, reality television, and the immediate release of downloads of television shows such as *Desperate Housewives*, challenged long-held assumptions. The publishing industry is still struggling to determine what the proliferation of electronic media means for their business models. Since no one knows for sure, I would bet on those new entrants who do things deemed foolish by the established houses.

- **Your experience with a problem is limited.** If you are unfamiliar with a problem, you should be more open-minded in approaching it. Suppose the organization is opening up a new office overseas or an entire new theme park, such as Disney did in France a few decades ago. It will be tempting to apply models or strategies borrowed from the home-market environment, as these lie within your comfort and experience zones.

  Disney did exactly this and ended up with a nearly bankrupt Disneyland Paris, also known as EuroDisney. It took senior management far too long to realize that the home-market model did not fit the new environment well. For example, EuroDisney did not serve alcohol in the new theme park and badly estimated how long parents would be willing to wait in lines for rides or spend on food and accessories.[74] Making deliberate mistakes at the outset—such as serving wine at EuroDisney—could help expedite the new learning that may be required to establish a beach-head in a new market.

In the 1980s, most large grocery stores had little experience with organic foods. Organic food sales were often relegated to separate natural food stores. It was presumed that only a small minority of shoppers were invested enough in the idea of organic to seek out these products. But suppose the large stores had made the mistake of dedicating large sections of their floor space to this growing market—or even establishing independent chains? This is essentially what Whole Foods Market did when it founded its first small store in Austin, Texas, in 1980. Now Whole Foods has more than 300 stores in North America and the United Kingdom, with a stock market value exceeding $11 billion. Whole Foods tapped into one of the fastest growing parts of the market and enjoyed 20% growth per annum for many years. Most traditional supermarkets are playing catch-up and expanding their organic food sections. Could these traditional players have learned faster by making a mistake in this organic arena before Whole Foods became a dominant player?

Exploring Your Willingness to Make Mistakes

In a world where outcomes are never certain, it could be argued that every action has the potential to be a mistake. Managers perform experiments all the time, both formally and informally, but it's important to distinguish between these experiments and real, deliberate mistakes. The critical distinction lies in the manager's expectation of success—not just the probability of good outcomes but positive expected payoff. I emphasize the latter criterion in order to cover experiments with very low probability of success but with payoff potential high enough to compensate for the risk. Running an experiment that costs $1 million, with a chance

of success of just 10% and a payoff of $15 million if success-
ful, does not qualify as a deliberate mistake. It is simply a
smart experiment with a positive expected value of $500,000,
namely 10% of $15 million minus $1 million. Furthermore,
the relevant yardstick need not be money—in principle, it
would include anything that falls under the economist's
notion of value or utility.

The term *utility* covers any potential decision outcome,
or payoff, that might produce pleasure or pain. Utility can be
measured in dollars and cents or by less tangible metrics, such
as impact on reputation of the firm, morale of employees,
or the risk of getting a regulatory fine. Utility, then, is the gold
standard against which we judge whether an action is a well-
advised experiment or a deliberate mistake. If an experiment
is *expected* to yield positive utility (compared to not doing
it), then it can be categorized as the former; if positive utility
is *not* expected, it is the latter. A very basic primer on expected
utility theory is offered in appendix B.

Integral to the notion of expected utility is the concept
of an individual's tolerance for risk. A proposed test may have
a positive expected utility for one person and a negative one
for another. The only difference could be each party's risk
tolerance. For example, you might reject the chance to flip a
coin for $100, whereas your friend might accept it. Assuming
that both of you agree on the possible outcomes (win $100
or lose $100) and the relevant probabilities (a 50-50 bet),
your opposite choices simply reflect differences in your risk
attitude. You may each have made the right decision given
your tolerance for gambling.

In sum, the definition of a deliberate mistake is an action
that is perceived—when viewed within an analytic mode of
thinking—to yield less expected utility than not conducting
the test. The only reason managers might conduct such
mistakes is that they recognize that "normal mode of thinking"

may be flawed. The primary aim of deliberate mistakes, therefore, is to test the validity of hidden assumptions that are hard, if not impossible, to analyze within an expected utility framework. This is not an easy sell in rigid organizations but should be natural for those embracing innovation and learning.

Much has been written about organizations' resistance to change and experimentation of any kind—let alone deliberate mistake-making. A range of causes have been proposed for this resistance, from incentive structures to cultural norms to mental models. Regardless of the cause, it's well understood that challenging an organization's dominant logic is nearly impossible unless such inquiries have the support of senior leadership. Even if senior support exists, companies may still fail, as research on disruptive technologies has amply shown.[75] Precisely because managers follow sound practices and do everything right, they may embrace the current strategy for too long, like the cautious entrepreneurs who fail by going down with the sinking ship of their original business plans. In essence, such companies get trapped by the status quo bias. Once leaders acknowledge that their companies can fail even if they do everything right (as judged by the firm's dominant logic and past), it behooves them to do a few things wrong on purpose.

In striving to counter the status quo bias, leaders use a variety of methods and techniques, from skunk works to venture fairs to training and official experimentation.[76] Seldom do these approaches, however, rise to the level of deliberate mistakes. Most of these experiments can be justified within an expected utility framework. For example, a corporate venture fund might invest in risky or unproven ideas, but these typically have been vetted by a committee or at least approved by one champion from senior management. A mistake fund, in contrast, would allocate a small amount of seed funding to ideas championed by employees, recognizing that senior managers may not always have the right framework for assessing deviant investments. If these endeavors yield good results, they would challenge senior management's perspective and open new doors for success. Google comes perhaps closest to embracing such an approach.

In practice, most organizations are far less willing to experiment than they should be. Typically, an organization will have a few cloistered areas, like R&D or market research, where experimentation is tacitly permitted, but the rest of the employees are expected to operate in a manner that prioritizes performance far above learning. It takes remarkable organizational dexterity to strike a balance between these antithetical orientations. Testing deep assumptions in an intelligent way is a fine art, demanding great courage. Indeed, the more successful and celebrated you are, the more challenging it may be to examine your own assumptions and mental model. Yet such humility may be precisely the key to future success, since the world around you will surely change. The following quiz lets you assess if you (or your organization) are ready to embark on our counterintuitive path of discovery. Additional self-assessments can be found in Alina Tugend's excellent book *Better by Mistake* (2011). It includes an interesting test of perfectionism; those who score high fear error and often fail to learn as much as they can from mistakes.[77]

Ready for Deliberate Mistakes?

You can answer the questions from the perspective of yourself as a manager, your organizational unit, the organization as a whole, the CEO, or even the board. Score each question in the following way: 1 = definitely no; 4 = to some extent; 7 = definitely yes.

1. Do you think that many of your crucial beliefs about your business may in fact be wrong?
2. Did you ever do something against your better judgment just to see what would happen?

3. Have you ever given an award to someone who tried something new that did not work?
4. When confronted with puzzling data, do you naturally insist on multiple explanations?
5. Are you viewed as an innovator in your field—as someone who challenges received wisdom?
6. Have you systematically tried to identify your implicit business assumptions?
7. Are you tolerant of mavericks—that is, credible people who hold unusual or contrarian views?
8. Do you value a learning culture in addition to a performance culture?
9. Has your industry seen disruptive changes, with new business models arising?
10. Has past success made you complacent or perhaps even arrogant; is there hubris?

The higher your total score (with a max of 70), the more ready you are to start implementing our strategy of deliberate mistakes. If your score is very high (over 60), you may already be doing much of what I recommend in this book. If your score is low (less than 30), you need to practice what we preach. There's great opportunity ahead for you, even though it might seem daunting to set out on this new course. Ask people around you to read this chapter, and encourage internal debate. Line up top-level champions. Find those who will support these changes and reassure employees that they will not be punished for their mistakes.

An Open Mind Is a Fertile Mind

Many brilliant ideas look like mistakes at the outset. The standard brainstorming technique of first generating ideas (without prejudging their merit) and then evaluating them makes good sense. Cognitively, this is an efficient division of labor; your mind uses different areas when thinking expansively versus critically. Some organizations take this idea further, setting up brainstorming groups comprised of people known for their out-of-the-box thinking. Homeland Security, for example, has formed a group called Sigma, tapping into the wild imaginations of self-described deviant thinkers: science fiction writers. Sigma's objective is to advise government officials about the unthinkable.[78]

What might society look like after a nuclear holocaust? How might terrorists foil our national defense? As far-fetched as this might sound, the idea has a historical precedent: the science fiction writer H. G. Wells (1866–1946) envisioned atomic bombs, airplanes, televisions, and joystick controls decades in advance of their discovery. The Sigma group operates under the motto "Science Fiction in the National Interest" and views itself as "well-qualified nuts" who can anticipate the offbeat attack and/or a brilliant defense. Many of their ideas remain under wraps for security reasons, but the spirit is clear. When the subject of bomb-sniffing dogs came up, it did not take long for them to conjure up a doggie brain-scanning skullcap to diagnose what kind of explosives pooch had sniffed out.

Business is replete with examples of "mistaken" ideas that turned out to be brilliant (and not just due to dumb luck). The second column in the following table lists various past mistakes across diverse industries that turned out to be successful. At the time, many of these seemed to be folly, and their proponents were often ridiculed. This is just a small list of the numerous innovations that occurred over many centuries that proved past beliefs wrong. Indeed, by definition, an innovation challenges the received wisdom by offering a new way to achieve a desired end. In this spirit, and to add some spice, the third column offers some "silly" ideas that most industry leaders today would consider mistakes. Each idea here is meant to challenge conventional wisdom, as noted in the last column. We leave it those working in each industry to figure out which of these ideas are crazy, promising, or perhaps brilliant. Unfortunately, those who know the industry well may not be the best judge; often, brilliant innovations come from outside the industry.

Industry	Past Mistakes	Today's Mistakes	Conventional Wisdom
Automobile	Return to retro car styles (VW Beetle, PT Cruiser); Volvo emphasizing safety; Toyota increasing quality without increasing cost	Disposable cars, recyclable (eco-friendly), and priced so low that reliability is not an issue (for example, Tata Motors has launched a $2,500 car in India)	Reliability or quality is number one
Banking	Replace human tellers with technology (ATMs); instant loan approval; making loans to presumed bad risks (credit cards to college students, microlending)	Banks in vans— home delivery of cash and other banking services; totally virtual and paperless banks; wealth or income insurance (to guarantee preservation of capital or income)	A bank without a branch ain't a bank; investing is inherently risky (no guarantees)
Television, cable, and entertainment	Twenty-four-hour news; reality shows; talent competition; sleeper films such as *The Passion of the Christ*	Use multimedia blogging to replace expert newscasters with selections from amateurs' home-grown reports	The audience wants good-looking talking heads who are truly experts
Pets	Pet superstores, pet grooming, pet psychiatry, pet health insurance, pet cemeteries, and pet estate planning	Pet restaurants and drive-thrus	Pets rank lower than kids in terms of people's care and budget

Industry	Past Mistakes	Today's Mistakes	Conventional Wisdom
Airlines	Low-budget, point-to-point (Southwest); frequent flyer programs (American Airlines); massages in coach (Virgin); fractional private plane ownership	Door-to-door service, combining both air and ground, and vacation memories (download photos on way home); swinger flights and sin flights where anything goes	Airlines transport people from Point A to Point B as safely and cheaply as possible
Real estate developers	Modular and prefab housing; time-sharing	Use for-profit, Habitat for Humanity model for "build your own" low-cost housing	Only frontier folk build their own houses
Health care	HMOs; outpatient clinics; alternative medicines	Offer outsourced health care to Indian doctors for lower cost (by phone, Internet, or medical tourism)	Patients want local practitioners who are like them
Personal computer retailing	Eliminate inventory (Dell)	Give away the machine, make money on banner ads and subscriptions	You can't make money if you give it all away
Tobacco	Filtered cigarettes; tobacco-free cigarettes	Sell smokers' health insurance policies (to forestall lawsuits)	We are not in the health, but sin, business
Advertising	Product placement; buzz and viral marketing; celebrity endorsements (Tiger Woods)	Invest advertising budget into product development; offer free/low-cost cell phone service in exchange for cell phone ads	Advertising deserves its own identity, in budgets and otherwise
Recording industry	Downloading and sharing music files; sell albums digitally by the song	Give credit for trading in old songs (for example, returning unused portion of fixed downloads)	We *sell* music

Industry	Past Mistakes	Today's Mistakes	Conventional Wisdom
Food retailing	Convenience store (high-priced)	Inconvenience store—high price, poor locations—but high entertainment value and chic atmosphere (Starbucks of groceries)	Our thin margins wouldn't allow it (remember Virgin's massages at 30,000 feet and personal movie selection in coach)
Insurance	Sell competitors' products (Progressive); make a lizard your spokesperson (Geico); build a brand in a short time using a duck (Aflac)	Require customer training in decision making and risk reduction in exchange for lower fees; offer longevity insurance (to protect against outliving your assets)	The actuarial table is the altar at which we pray
Office equipment	Personal copier	Combination printer/copier/fax and karaoke machine—improving office culture and productivity	Let's not mix business and pleasure
Car rental	Focusing on off-airport locations (as Enterprise did)	Offer bundled car rental and driver (to serve elderly or business segment), more convenient and lower-cost than limos	It's all about feeder location (for example, airport), cars, prices, and brand
Military	Use of commercial technology on battlefield (soldiers using BlackBerrys); in Iraq, commanders would rather have more PCs than bullets	Let amateurs design unmanned battlefield vehicles through prize competition. DARPA's first desert rally had no finishers (all mistakes), the next year all contestants finished the race	Sophisticated military hardware should be left to the military experts

Industry	Past Mistakes	Today's Mistakes	Conventional Wisdom
Space travel	Moon launch; communications satellites	Commercial space travel and mining natural resources (precious metals in meteorites)	It's too early, expensive, and risky to mine space
Education	Nondegree courses and continuing education	Revoke degrees that are out of date or require periodic updates	A degree is a degree is a degree (it is a timeless, immutable certification)

Column Legend

- **Past "Mistakes":** Novel ideas at the time that really violated the conventional wisdom and proved to be brilliant when launched
- **Today's "Mistakes":** Novel ideas that violate today's conventional wisdom and will likely be dismissed as idiotic but that may actually turn out to be brilliant (this list is of course speculative, and the author does not offer a money-back guarantee).
- **Conventional Wisdom:** A widely held current assumption that prevents the idea to the left from being taken seriously by the majority of industry experts; this may in the future be marked as a blind spot.

CHAPTER 6

Portfolio of Mistakes
Hedging Conventional Wisdom

Never test the depth of a river with both feet.
—African Proverb[79]

In the last chapter, I presented the case for purposeful, deliberate mistake-making to accelerate learning and gain a competitive edge in an uncertain world. In this chapter, I take this idea a step further and argue for the wisdom of making *multiple* mistakes as a way of hedging against over-reliance on conventional wisdom. I present the virtues of a bold, experimental approach to mistake-making in your personal life, family, and organization and in society at large. As the African proverb at the start of the chapter counsels, the wise person never jumps into any assumption with total abandon. Keep one foot grounded in the familiar, especially if the river you are testing with the other foot is wide, deep, quickly moving, or simply unknown.

At first blush, the notion of engaging in multiple errors may sound radical. It may make you nervous, or it just may not feel right. If one mistake can turn out badly, don't multiple mistakes carry the risk of things turning out . . . well, *very* badly? Not necessarily. The secret is diversifying your risk. As we established in previous chapters, mistakes are like financial investments—they entail inherent risks while offering the potential payoff of new insights and opportunities. The underlying logic of a financial portfolio is that spreading your risk across multiple baskets reduces your total downside exposure. The basic idea behind this diversification strategy is simple: do not put all your eggs in one basket. The same applies to mistakes. Just as with financial options, it's wise to establish a varied portfolio of potential failures so that a few may turn out to be brilliant mistakes.

The Benefits of a Portfolio

If you accept the premise that mistakes, like financial investments, must be spread across multiple baskets, a practical question remains. How, exactly, do you put this idea into practice? You could turn to a financial adviser or study up on the markets to understand how to manage a financial portfolio. But what principles apply when thinking about a portfolio of mistakes? How much diversification is optimal, and what would a proper degree of diversification even look like in real life?

Let's start with a simple real-world example: a family who is planning an overseas vacation. Perhaps they are somewhat anxious, so they think about actions to take that would minimize catastrophic losses. The parents decide to fly in separate planes to ensure the kids don't end up as orphans. Also, they resolve to divide up their cash so that if one person is pickpocketed, they will not end up having to beg for cab fare back to their hotel. You might look at this family and argue that through their actions, they have *doubled* the chances of something bad happening. (You might also speculate whether their extreme tactics might be frightening their children—but that would belong in another book.) But if a mishap were to occur, this family's loss is limited to about half of the total potential loss.

This example relies, of course, on the idea that both parents are equally careful and don't diverge in their propensities to be unlucky or dumb. In real life—as with financial investments—nothing is ever that clear and distinct. The prudence levels of the parents are likely to vary—perhaps one parent is the sort that tends to misplace keys, linger in dark bars, or flash money around on crowded subway platforms. Moreover, the risks these parents face might not be independent—a rash of pickpockets in the city they are visiting would affect them both, just as a recession adversely affects most of the stock returns across a portfolio. In the language of portfolio theory, you need to account for the *correlations* among the various investments. Finance folks refer to this as the covariance matrix, and this is what allows the investor to devise a clever portfolio. Appendix C argues more formally that an investment offering a negative expected return may still be attractive when viewed within a portfolio context. But if so, it must exhibit sufficient negative correlation with the other investments in your portfolio.

Also, the assumption is made in portfolio theory that the investor is risk-averse. When applying these insights to your own life, you need to consider what your own risk attitude actually is. You might be the type who likes to have all of your assets in one basket so that you can watch that basket like a hawk. Or you might prefer to spread your wealth across many baskets and accept the fact that you won't be able to pay as close attention to each as you might like. If so, you are increasing the chance that you might suffer *some* loss but with the benefit of less risk that you might lose it all. The more risk-averse you are, the more you should wish to diversify your investments—to the point of making deliberate mistakes. It may seem rather counterintuitive that the more risk-averse you are, the more you should make mistakes on purpose as a hedge against the wisdom of the crowd's being wrong. But that is clearly what portfolio theory implies (as shown in appendix C).

Portfolio Thinking Goes Against the Grain

Despite its inherent logic, portfolio thinking seems to go
against the human grain. It requires that we look at problems
not in isolation but in aggregate. As simple as it sounds, this
is not something the human mind does naturally. It is much
easier to solve one problem at a time than to solve multiple
problems simultaneously. We all suffer from limited attention
and memory capacity. It's easier to keep problems within
separate boxes; it makes the problems easier to comprehend.

To illustrate, imagine that I invite you to make two decisions. The first decision requires you to choose between
options where you stand to win some money. Specifically, I
offer you $240 cash in hand, or you can spin a wheel of
chance that offers you a 25% chance of getting $1,000 and a
75% of you leaving empty-handed. While you try to make
up your mind, however, I tell you that you'll need to make a
second decision as well—this time involving losses. You must
let me reach into your piggybank and take $750. Alterna-
tively, you can spin another wheel of chance in which there
is a 25% chance that you will lose nothing but a 75% chance
that I will take even more—in this case, $1,000.

Confused? I will make it simple for you. I will hand you
this chart:

Decision 1: Choose A or B
A) Sure gain of $240
B) 25% chance of gaining $1,000 and a
    75% of getting $0

Decision 2: Choose C or D
C) Sure loss of $750
D) 75% chance of losing $1,000 and a
    25% chance of losing $0

So: what will you decide? If you are like most people, you will choose A in situation 1 and D in situation 2. This means that you will take the $240 cash in hand, and then you'll take your chances in terms of escaping any loss. That sounds right, doesn't it?

Unfortunately, you wouldn't have made the wisest decision, given this set of circumstances. If you consider the problem from a portfolio viewpoint, you would recognize that you face not two but *four* choices: AC, AD, BC, and BD. As shown in figure 6-1, the payoffs of these four choice profiles differ significantly. The one that most people choose—AD—is inferior to the combination BC. Although the probabilities don't differ across these two profiles, combination AD offers less reward ($240 versus $250) and more potential loss than BC (-$760 versus -$750). In choosing AD, you've suboptimized your chance of walking away from me with the most money left in your hands.

Fig 6-1 Did You Take a Portfolio Perspective?

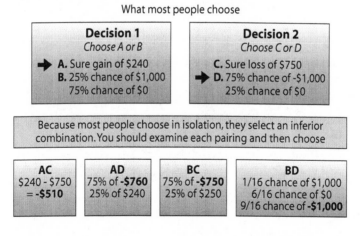

What most people choose

Decision 1 *Choose A or B*	Decision 2 *Choose C or D*
➡ **A.** Sure gain of $240 **B.** 25% chance of $1,000 75% chance of $0	**C.** Sure loss of $750 ➡ **D.** 75% chance of -$1,000 25% chance of $0

Because most people choose in isolation, they select an inferior combination. You should examine each pairing and then choose

AC	AD	BC	BD
$240 - $750 = **-$510**	75% of **-$760** 25% of $240	75% of **-$750** 25% of $250	1/16 chance of $1,000 6/16 chance of $0 9/16 chance of **-$1,000**

Don't despair if you chose poorly: very few people naturally look at the two decisions, and their outcomes, simultaneously. Instead, most of us examine each choice in isolation from the other. Psychologists Kahneman and Tversky used this example to demonstrate what they termed the *isolation effect*: our tendency to look at problems one at a time without thinking much about the combined effect of our choices.[80] We encounter this problem as well when thinking about mistakes. The lesson is clear: a portfolio of mistakes, if wisely managed and understood as being interdependent, offers greater opportunity for a positive payoff than a mistake made in isolation. The next question then becomes: which *portfolio* mistakes should you create in order to test key assumptions?

Research in portfolio theory has amply proved the benefits of diversification and hedging in financial investments. Let's apply these same ideas to mistakes. As with investments, the trick is to increase your expected payoff while limiting the downside potential of loss. You want to deliberately create the right risk balance in your mistake portfolio. This approach becomes especially appealing if the various eggs in your portfolio basket are not statistically independent but negatively correlated. Once you understand the degree of inverse correlation with other bets you can invest in, you can start to *hedge*. Hedging means placing bets that yield a payoff when things don't go as hoped for. We engage in hedging all the time in terms of self-protection; it's the seat belt you buckle when driving, the extra parachute you strap on before leaping from the plane. The aim is to design a well-hedged portfolio such that if one component declines, it will be partly offset by the rise of another component.

Brilliant mistakes offer the biggest hedge of all, since they typically have the highest negative correlation with conventional wisdom. The more the consensus view turns out to be correct (something that it's impossible to know ahead of time), the less likely it is that your deliberate mistakes will succeed. Conversely, however, when the prevailing views in a society or an organization are wrong, there is a greater chance that a deviant act will produce surprise and new insight. Since most of us are heavily vested in the conventional wisdom of our culture—in terms of how we live, work, and invest—it pays to "place a bet" on a mistake.

Placing Many Small Bets: The Portfolio Approach

This kind of hedging approach was successfully used by the Pentagon's DARPA in developing robot vehicles. Congress passed a mandate requiring that at least a third of DARPA's military ground vehicles be unmanned by 2015. Given this intense pressure, you might expect DARPA to seek out the most experienced people and companies in the world to help design and develop prototypes. But they didn't. Instead they made the "mistake" of turning to amateurs. In 2004, they invited inventors and entrepreneurial engineers of all stripes to come up with designs for unmanned vehicles and bring their products to Nevada for a race across the desert. They offered the winner a $1 million prize.

DARPA was well aware that their process would invite many failures. The first time around, in 2004, the outcomes were indeed dismal. The competitors barely made it off the starting line. It would have been easy, at this point, to drop the entire concept and turn to acknowledged experts, but DARPA pressed on. They repeated the contest the next year and even increased the prize money to $2 million—essentially, in gamblers' terms, doubling down on their original bet. In the 2005 race, five vehicles finished the 142-mile course. A modified Volkswagen Touareg created by a team from Stanford University took the prize. This was real progress; it put DARPA on a path to meet the congressional mandate. By explicitly encouraging a high failure rate through the mistake of using amateurs, DARPA was able to build a portfolio that contained many mistakes and a few successes.

A similar approach was pursued recently at DEFCON, a well-known computer and security conference operating on the dark side of the Internet. It was started by amateur hackers in 1992 and has become the world's longest-running and largest underground expert hacking conference.[81] It is now attended as well by corporate IT specialists, programmers, and software companies. At previous DEFCONs, hackers and the technology specialists whose job it is to monitor and mitigate their damage gathered to share tactics and ideas. At the most recent DEFCON, organizers invited teens and even preteens to participate. It would seem to be a mistake to allow children into this sophisticated conference. The organizers must have worried that older hackers would feel condescended to or that the serious results they had come to expect from previous years would be diluted. But in the end they were intrigued by the emergence of some truly brilliant, very young hackers.

For example, a 10-year-old girl who goes by the cyberspace name of CyFi managed to break into the mobile game FarmVille to speed up its slow, meandering story line. To do so, she had hacked into Android and iOS platforms—previously believed to be impenetrable—and changed FarmVille's clock speed. At DEFCON, CyFi presented her strategy to an audience of 100, without identifying her specific targets. She thereby gave game makers fair warning that they were vulnerable to attack. And it isn't just game manufacturers who keep an eye on DEFCON's proceedings: government agencies, like NASA and Homeland Security, have expressed interest in connecting with DEFCON. They want to learn the latest tricks and also hope to persuade talented youngsters to apply their special programming gifts to more positive ends than hacking. In particular, the highly secretive National Security Agency (NSA) attended the most recent DEFCON and shortly thereafter announced plans to hire 1,500 cyber experts to combat computer fraud and hacking.

Both the DARPA and DEFCON examples demonstrate how an ecosystem of mistakes, or portfolio of risks, can generate a few successes. DARPA could have followed a more directed and logical design approach by turning to the top research labs. Instead, it used an unmanned approach, a mad road race that tapped into new sources of innovation. Similarly, DEFCON might have restricted attendance to adult hackers, but allowing in children lent the conference both content richness and public interest, generating additional publicity and funding.

Managing Diversity: The Key to Portfolio Thinking

In proposing a portfolio approach, I first argued that diversification is a good way to manage overall risk. Then, we explored some examples—an imaginary one (the two decisions game) and two "real" ones (DARPA and DEFCON)—as illustrations of how portfolio principles can raise the mean level of performance while reducing unnecessary risk. As noted, portfolio models are commonly used in finance to better balance risk and return. However, its central premises extend already well beyond finance, into strategy (product and market portfolio) as well as innovation (growth options and pipelines). By extension, portfolio thinking applies to making mistakes as well. At any given point in time, we need to expose ourselves to enough experiments, including deliberate mistakes, to accelerate our learning curve.[82]

In addition to diversifying a portfolio in terms of the "risk profile" of each element, it is also wise to diversify in terms of the timelines of expected outcomes. This kind of longitudinal hedging is especially crucial in industries with long innovation pipelines, such as pharmaceutical companies. The robustness of the product pipeline of a pharmaceutical company is evaluated not just by the potential of the products it offers today but in terms of the long-term opportunities it has in production, at various stages in the R&D and FDA approval process.

Taking this idea further, companies should define their portfolios not just in product terms but also in terms of geographic regions of the world (their global footprint), their organizational competencies (talent pools), technology platforms, alliances or networks, cultural values, and indeed any form of asset that can bestow firm value. In other words, *a portfolio of mistakes should aim for diversity along multiple dimensions.* As depicted in figure 6-2, companies need a balanced set of intelligent experiments, including some deliberate mistakes, so as to open surprising portals of discovery. For example, when exploring new terrain (markets, products, technologies, regions), how can portfolio thinking help? How can companies devise long-term strategies where the learning from one project sets up discovery opportunities for the next one?[83] As with venture capital funds and real options portfolios in general, just a few projects in the mistakes portfolio are expected to yield returns high enough to compensate for the many that fail.

Fig 6-2 Designing Your Mistakes Portfolio

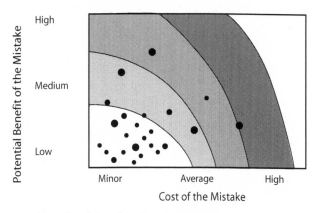

Note: Size of dot reflects investment amount

In designing mistake portfolios, one of the main challenges is the almost unlimited number of assumptions that one could, in theory, test. Unlike stocks in a financial portfolio, where you can easily get in and out of any one investment, the options in a mistake portfolio take time and effort to explore. This places importance on selection criteria and the process used to narrow the targets. A detailed, intelligent set of filters can help you be selective about which ideas to pursue.

The tournament or contest model is one method that some organizations (like DARPA, as we saw) have used to guide the mistake-making process through appropriate filters.[84] The basic advantage of a tournament is that it draws in numerous candidates and offers clear guidelines by which a small set of winners are moved on to the next round, where they compete further for survival. Just as in a tennis tournament, losers get eliminated in successive rounds until only a few remain. As the book *Innovation Tournaments* explains, the key is to manipulate several variables that can enhance your chance of identifying a few winners out of 10,000 or more candidates, as in drug discovery, for example.[85]

The first obvious lever is to raise the unknown mean of the ideas submitted, by tapping into higher-caliber people or by using proven idea generation techniques such as brainstorming or synectics. A second, more subtle lever is to increase the variance of ideas submitted. You will need to accept that many of these additional ideas may be really bad ones, as the organization casts a wider net. But a few of them may be turn out to be brilliant, as in the DARPA example. A third lever is to refine the screens used at each stage to flush out bad ideas and perhaps allow limited reentry if some earlier rejects improved themselves. A fourth lever is creating and exploiting correlations among the submitted ideas, as in traditional portfolio modeling. This means welcoming contrarian ideas into the competition and betting on subsets that you expect to exhibit inverse correlations. Clearly, there is considerable science—as well as managerial art—to optimizing the order statistics underlying this kind of sequential tournament.

The idea that randomly increasing the range of observation can increase the chance of discovery is well appreciated in science. The biologist and Nobel Laureate Max Delbrück (1906-1981) advocated strongly for "the principle of limited sloppiness." He advised his students to be sloppy enough in their lab experiments to allow for the unexpected but not so sloppy that they could not identify the reasons for their anomalous results.[86] Alexander Fleming's discovery of penicillin—as discussed in the next chapter—is an instructive example of the power of limited sloppiness. This principle doesn't mean that you should go out and make really stupid mistakes. The trick is to make wise mistakes, ones that produce the most learning and manageable pain. But, as discussed in chapter 2, you will have to tolerate some level of dumb mistakes in order to produce a few brilliant ones. So, in essence, you face a portfolio balancing problem whenever you pursue a brilliant mistake strategy. If you play it safe, you will make few errors and learn little new. If you swing for the fences, you may knock yourself out of business. The number of swings at bat, and knowing whether to aim for the bleachers, are essential in determining your optimal mistake portfolio.

To summarize: there is both art and science to making informative errors, and adopting a portfolio perspective can change the way we consider failure. If you embrace the broad perspective and the long view, you can afford to take on far more risk than you had previously imagined. In doing so, it's important to remember some core lessons:

1. Because deliberate mistakes entail low-probability, high-payoff bets, with some degree of inverse correlation, a portfolio approach can help improve the overall risk-return profile of a brilliant mistake strategy.

2. Deliberate mistakes can help you hedge against the blinkering effects of received wisdom. They are best thought of in terms of portfolio counterbalancing. Their negative correlation with conventional wisdom would be reason alone to invest some resources away from the crowd.

3. The most powerful argument for deliberate mistakes is the simplest: the wisdom of testing beyond the boundaries of your deepest assumptions.

Part Three
Putting It All Together

CHAPTER 7

The Prepared Mind
Detecting Anomalies

Chance only favors the prepared mind.
—LOUIS PASTEUR[87]

Deep new insights are usually the end result of a long period of gestation. A novel idea traverses a slow, convoluted path from initial brain wave to innovative action. The creative process has preoccupied many of the best thinkers; nevertheless, some of its critical elements remain shrouded in mystery.[88] Creativity is difficult to model, as it tends to be catalyzed by chance occurrences and micro interactions that cannot be identified, let alone orchestrated precisely, ahead of time.

There is, however, one key element that *has* been identified as critical to the nonlinear creative process: keen observation. Those with great experience in a field tend to notice things that others may miss, including the surprising or indirect consequences of mistakes. Louis Pasteur makes the point concisely: the mind itself must be consciously prepared, deliberately receptive, in order for serendipity to do its "magical" work. In this chapter, I make the case for Pasteur's point, demonstrating that chance favors the mind that is not simply "prepared" but which actively plumbs, and seeks to falsify, widely held beliefs. Figure 7-1 summarizes the basic logic flow of brilliant mistakes.

To illustrate the complexities of brilliant discovery, this chapter explores a legendary story of the evolution of a peripheral idea into one of medicine's most remarkable

Fig 7-1 Pathway of a Brilliant Mistake

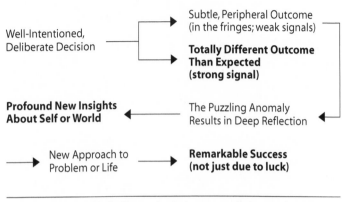

Note: The essence of a brilliant mistake is someone's deep realization,
occasioned by an unexpected outcome following a decision made, that
the above loop is important in breaking wrong mental models, and
therefore, more such loops need to be created on purpose.

miracle drugs. We will follow the twists, turns, and unusual
confluences of circumstance that allowed the brilliant,
unconventional Scottish scientist Alexander Fleming to
discover the wonder drug penicillin.[89] This intriguing story
demonstrates the importance of deep scientific training,
careful observation, openness to new ideas, and a playful as
well as an inquiring mind-set. In the previous chapter, I mentioned biologist Max Delbrück, who argued for the virtues
of what he termed "the principle of limited sloppiness."
Fleming's story, as we'll see, reveals the quintessential power
of limited and deliberate sloppiness.

A Nobel from the Trash

In September 1928, Fleming discovered a culture dish
containing staphylococcus bacteria in his lab at Saint Mary's
College in London. This mundane discovery on a seemingly
ordinary day would change the course of medicine.

Fleming was known as a brilliant but somewhat careless researcher. Typically, his lab was chaotic; this day was no exception. He had just returned from a long vacation and was entertaining a visitor. The culture dishes were filled with mold. In those days, culture dishes were glass plates that were cleaned and then reused. Fleming assumed that the cultures in them were now worthless and threw the dishes into disinfectant. However, he decided to show the visitor evidence of the work he was doing, so he pulled a few dishes back out of the liquid. He noticed something strange in one of the dishes: there was a halo where the fungus appeared to have dissolved the bacteria. This was no ordinary day after all.

Fleming's extraction of the culture dish that day was not the result of a carefully scripted experiment—it had the slightly random, opportunistic quality of a mistake. It had become contaminated (a common incident, in most labs). It had then festered for a long period before being cleaned (a less common incident in most labs, but a relatively frequent one in Fleming's workplace). It seemed destined to be buried with all the other routine minor mistakes of lab work. But Fleming took notice of the critical difference between this contaminated dish and the countless others that had passed through his hands over the course of his career. This seeming mistake ultimately catalyzed one of the most extraordinary medical breakthroughs of the 20th century: the discovery of penicillin. This antibiotic ended up saving countless lives, and Fleming was eventually awarded the Nobel Prize for his research.

Let's pause for a moment and peer into that fateful petri dish. What else can these microbes teach us? Our first lesson is that ordinary mistakes, like Fleming's sloppiness, are not always bad. By blurring the margins of rules and discipline, they can lead us in new and exciting directions. The second and, arguably, more significant one is that mental preparation is critical to one's ability to learn. Many scientists would have likely overlooked the odd, intriguing growth pattern that Fleming noticed. He was innately curious and had developed a kind of obsession with bacterial reproduction. The third is that a single mistake, taken in isolation, is usually not enough to allow for the kind of circumstances that lead to ground-breaking insight like the discovery of the cure for a major disease. A series of mistakes, occurring across time, may be needed to create the type of outliers that serve as portals of new discovery—a rare multiplicative conjunction of events in a low-probability chain. As momentous as Fleming's moment with the contaminated dish was, it's unlikely that it would have occurred without other, necessary steps preceding.

To fully appreciate how multiple errors can spark a prepared mind to new insight, it pays to dive deeper into Fleming's background. He was born on a farm in Scotland and spent the early part of his career in a shipping office. After receiving an inheritance from an uncle in 1901, he enrolled in St. Mary's Hospital in London, intending to become a doctor like his older brother Tom. At the urging of a friend, he joined the research department instead, serving as assistant bacteriologist to Sir Almroth Wright, a pioneer in vaccine therapy and immunology. When World War I broke out, Fleming went to the battlefield in Germany as a member of the Army Medical Corps. Serving as a captain in battlefield hospitals, Fleming witnessed the deaths of many soldiers due to septicemia. He made an appalling observation: many of the current antiseptics were effective on the skin but killed more soldiers than the diseases themselves when used on deep battlefield wounds. He returned to St. Mary's with a mission: the search for antibacterial agents. In 1922, Fleming discovered lysozyme, known as the "body's own antibiotic." This remarkable discovery preceded the discovery of penicillin six years later. Like the later discovery, it was part accident and part design.

As a child, Fleming had broken his nose. Due to this early injury, he suffered frequent colds, and London labs were poorly heated. On a chilly afternoon in 1922, Fleming's nose dripped into his petri dish. With his customary curiosity, Fleming observed that some, but not all, of the colonies splashed by the mucus melted away. On closer observation, he ascertained that the colonies affected were not ones that he had deliberately cultivated but others that had been introduced by contamination. His curiosity piqued, Fleming subcultured these foreign colonies on additional plates and then purposely introduced more nasal mucus. Again, he observed that the bacteria were melting away. Thanks to these two interrelated errors—the use of contaminated plates and the introduction of drops of nasal mucus—Fleming discovered lysozyme, a catalytic protein with antibacterial properties. It is now known that lysozyme, together with the skin, lymphocytes, and antibodies, is one of the body's four major defense mechanisms against infection. It is present in virtually all tissues and body excretions. Previous to Fleming's discovery, it was not known that this fourth line of defense even existed, so it had never been pursued through any specific line of inquiry. Since conventional medical wisdom believed that there were just *three* lines of defense against infection, it took a brilliant mistake for a new insight to emerge and challenge the dominant paradigm.

Michelangelo of the Microbes

Scholars still debate the extent to which Fleming's discovery was due to strategy or chance.[90] Some speculate that Fleming's permissive attitude toward his petri dishes, which allowed them to become contaminated, was actually part of a deliberate effort to study a broad range of microbes. It's unlikely that firm consensus will ever be found on this question. It's also worth noting that such an unconventional approach would be fully in keeping with Fleming's personality and upbringing. Fleming was eccentric, even by British standards. This is an important factor in understanding his remarkable discoveries.

Fleming's family loved games and had little respect for rules and boundaries. On the golf course, he was known for his thoroughly unconventional maneuvers, such as putting the ball like a pool player sinking a shot into the corner pocket. Fleming ribbed a fellow scientist who dutifully put his lab bench in order every night about his excessive tidiness. As the penicillin discovery story makes clear, Fleming did just the opposite, keeping cultures for several weeks before discarding them. Whether or not he was consciously practicing "controlled sloppiness," Fleming was always curious to see if something unexpected happened in these dishes. His passion, curiosity, and irreverence also extended beyond the laboratory. He was a member of the Chelsea Art Club, founded by painter James McNeill Whistler. But instead of painting on canvas with oil, Fleming produced artwork drawn with a culture loop using spores of highly pigmented bacteria. With a similar irreverence, he treated his petri dishes like canvases; he would shape bacterial colonies to resemble animals as well as portraits of his colleagues.

Undeniably, this Michelangelo of microbes was a scientist who thought outside of the petri dish. His playful and unconventional demeanor, in concert with his childlike curiosity and deep scientific training, created a very prepared mind capable of expanding the normal range of observation. Was it the perspective of an artist that helped him see the penicillin? Did his odd bacterial painting skills give him an especially keen eye for even small irregularities in the shape of microbial colonies? Clearly, Fleming explored broadly and tried many things. But he also needed to have the ability to recognize a breakthrough when he saw it—to learn from his mistakes and experiments—and engage others in forging solutions. Six years after the lysozyme discovery, on a fateful day in 1928 when staphylococcus bacteria appeared in his petri dishes, Fleming was exceptionally well primed to recognize the incident as something larger than a simple lab error.

From Epiphany to Utility

Medicine was not transformed overnight by Fleming's discovery. Many years passed before the medical community fully recognized its brilliance and applicability. After noticing the effect of the blue-green mold on the bacteria, Fleming cultivated the mold in a separate culture, creating a filtrate that he named "penicillin." At that moment, he presumed that the substance wouldn't last long enough in the human body to be valuable as an antibiotic agent. So, in 1931, Fleming turned his focus away from the study of penicillin, although he would continue to dabble with the substance until around 1940. He encouraged other researchers to experiment further and find ways to make penicillin more useful in treatment. A few picked up the challenge. In 1939, Australian scientist Howard Walter Florey at the University of Oxford showed that the drug was safe but ineffective in mice. Florey's trials also failed in humans because his experiments involved doses of penicillin that were too low to be effective—another mistake on the road to discovery. Next, Ernst Chain, a gifted German scientist working with Florey at Oxford, correctly hypothesized the molecular structure of penicillin. This allowed him to isolate and concentrate the drug, thereby developing a more effective dosage. In 1940, the Chain-Florey team published their first results.

At that point, a full decade had passed since Fleming's eureka moment in the lab. In fact, when Fleming arrived in Chain's lab to see his results firsthand, Chain exclaimed: "I thought you were dead!"[91] Fleming was alive and well, and his original discovery was on the brink of enormous medical success. With a more concentrated drug, scientists closed in on human applications. In 1942, at the Radcliffe Infirmary in Oxford, doctors John Bumstead and Orvan Hess became the first to successfully treat a human with penicillin. After fourteen years of failures—finally, a brilliant result!

During World War II, penicillin saved an estimated 15 to 20% of injured soldiers who would otherwise have perished from infections. It is both the most widely used antibiotic in history and the foundation of the entire field of modern antibiotics. Penicillin has proved highly effective in treating staphylococcus bacteria and Gram-positive pathogens including those that cause scarlet fever, pneumonia, gonorrhea, meningitis, and diphtheria. Fleming was knighted in 1944. In 1945, he shared the Nobel Prize in Physiology or Medicine for the achievement with Florey and Chain. The world recognized that Fleming's habit of contaminating petri dishes turned out to be a brilliant mistake, or perhaps a brilliant research strategy, for humankind.

Flashes of Brilliance

Fleming's case is not unique. Many other scientific breakthroughs, from Minkowski's analysis of diabetes to Richet's examination of anaphylaxis, follow a similar pattern. These striking discoveries exhibit a rich and complex multi-causal character, occurring in environments that favored serendipity, either by design or by happenstance.[92] Opportunity is the combination of chance and a prepared mind. Genius, in turn, is primarily the result of extensive application of time and energy—on the order of many decades' worth—to prepare the mind for great discovery.

Fleming's brilliant insights entailed considerable serendipity. As noted earlier, it's an open question whether his "sloppy" research habits (like allowing plates to pile up, leaving the window open, or creating "art" from bacteria) were sufficiently aberrant to merit special notice. Likewise, we can debate whether Fleming's eye was unusually well trained to spot anomalous growth patterns, or whether other microbiologists, if presented with the same fleeting evidence, would also have noticed the deviant pattern.

It's possible that Fleming's most salient quality was his peripheral vision. Out of the corner of his eye, while entertaining a visitor, Fleming picked up an unexpected detail about the plates he was tossing into the sink. We might speculate that this superior peripheral vision, honed by many years of studying glass plates with bacterial growth, was responsible for this flash of brilliance. However one wishes to dissect this complex case, it is clear that the discovery of penicillin entailed a special mix of chance, error, and a prepared mind.

Peripheral Vision

As demonstrated by the Fleming case and other examples we discussed in previous chapters, a striking feature of the prepared mind is that it can recognize anomalies or weak signals that others fail to notice. Weak signals are easy to miss because they lurk in an area outside of where people focus their attention—they reside in the periphery. In our 2006 book *Peripheral Vision*, George Day and I discuss how individuals and organizations can hone their capacity to pick up weak signals from the edge.[93] We define a weak signal as a seemingly random or disconnected piece of information that appears, at first, to be mere background noise. But when examined through a different frame, it can be seen as part of a larger, significant pattern. The greatest challenge to sharpening your peripheral vision is acquiring that different frame—learning to process information through a different mental lens rather than the standby, familiar context. It is only then that you can connect the dots to form new, illuminating patterns.

Consider a striking historical example of missed signals at the start of the Second World War.[94] On the morning of December 7, 1941, the captain of the destroyer USS *Ward* heard muffled explosions coming from Pearl Harbor on the main island of Hawaii. Just before surfacing, this captain had dropped depth charges on what was presumed to be a foreign submarine moving into the harbor. While sailing back to port, the captain heard the muffled explosions of the first air attacks of the now-legendary Pearl Harbor onslaught. He turned to his lieutenant commander on deck and said, "I guess they are blasting the new road from Pearl Harbor to Honolulu."

The captain used his peacetime mind-set to make sense of the sound of explosions. He interpreted the loud explosions as part of road building, and thus failed to notice the signs of the first hostilities between the United States and Japan. Despite his unusual encounter with a foreign submarine that morning, his mind still defaulted to the familiar context of peace. The captain heard the explosion loud and clear, and he knew that a foreign submarine had made it into the harbor. Nevertheless, he lacked the clarity and lack of bias of a sufficiently prepared mind—and thereby lost the opportunity to connect the dots in a different, better way.

As strange as it sounds, the only way out of this trap is to try to make *less* sense of our surrounding world. When faced with new information, resist the impulse to jump to a conclusion and lock into one single view. Instead, step away and search for alternative perspectives. Some practical ways to do this are by being playful and curious (like Fleming), seeking alternative answers, and challenging your own assumptions. Peripheral signals don't call attention to themselves. You have to hunt for them like clues in a puzzle. You need to have a sufficiently prepared mind.

The philosopher Immanuel Kant emphasized that there can be no *perception* without *preception*.[95] I am referring to mental precepts, the set of preconceptions we all hold about the tenets of our surrounding environment. Precepts often act as filters. In a classic experiment by psychologist Jerome Bruner and colleagues, subjects are shown several playing cards from a deck for just 10 seconds and then asked to remember what they saw.[96] One of the cards shown has the wrong color, such as a red spade or a black heart. Very few people pick up on this anomaly. Simply put: in most situations, people see what they expect to see and filter out data that does not fit with their dominant mental framework. In life, as in card experiments, we distort the information we receive to make it align with our preconceived notions.

Kant's concern about mental preconceptions prompted the philosopher Hegel to propose a dialectical approach to truth seeking. He suggested that individuals strive to create deliberate tension between one hypothesis (the thesis) and an opposite one (the antithesis). This dialectical approach is routinely practiced in the US courtroom, where two opposing views battle for supremacy, allowing a jury to consider both perspectives before deciding where the truth lies. The Hegelian approach to truth-seeking seeks to create *inquiring systems* that allow the mind to see multiple sides of a complex issue.[97]

How do these lessons apply to individuals and organizations in today's world of management? One proven managerial technique to encourage collective mind expansion and dialectical thinking is *scenario planning*.[98] For example, in the midst of Enron's meteoric rise, our company got hired by a Houston-based credit union interested in strategic planning. Enron happened to be the sole corporate sponsor for this credit union—a situation that was quite common during that era. Thanks to Enron's success, this credit union was experiencing exponential growth. As an exercise, we asked the credit union's leaders to imagine a scenario in which they could no longer rely on Enron's generous deposits. At first, there was reluctance to entertain and develop such a pessimistic view. Some of the credit union's leaders seem to feel that even entertaining such a thought would somehow jinx their primary corporate relationship. But Roch Parayre, the senior partner leading the project, insisted that they give the exercise a try.

Some interesting ideas emerged, ranging from a takeover of the credit union *by* Enron to more dire scenarios involving trouble for either Enron or its credit union. (None of the imagined scenarios, it's worth noting, even came close to envisioning the eventual, apocalyptic end-of-story for Enron: its dissolution in scandal in 2001.) Parayre then asked how the credit union would respond *today* if they knew that some of these negative scenarios would, in fact, come to pass. Again, with some reluctance, the senior team obliged. They mentioned such "mistakes" as decoupling their email system from Enron's corporate system and opening branches outside of Enron's office buildings. They even mentioned changing the credit union's charter to a SEG (Select Employee Group program) so that other members, besides Enron employees, could join.

Exploring these scenarios as real possibilities shifted the mind-set of the leaders. They came to accept that the idea losing at least *some* measure of Enron's support was not entirely far-fetched. More significantly, they also came to see that some of the ideas they had generated in response to these scenarios were both practical and feasible and could be undertaken as a way to hedge against the unlikely (as it seemed at the time) possibility of Enron's decline. The credit union actually went so far as to implement several of these ideas. Later, when Enron collapsed nearly overnight, the credit union was saved—against the odds, according to regulators—because they had developed a strategy beyond

Enron. This strategy, of course, seems positively prescient in retrospect. At the moment they had created it and set it into motion, however, it felt very different—it looked like a deliberate mistake.

There are other tools that can help prepare our minds to see weak signals sooner, as summarized in figure 7-2. The more organizations practice these techniques, the greater the chance they will notice the often hidden or indirect consequence of mistakes made in the normal course of business. Managers will more readily spot any surprise or deviation from expectation, whether good or bad. The broader theme in developing better peripheral vision is to notice surprise, share it with others, and explore it deeply. This entails cognitive, organizational, and cultural challenges. Figure 7-2 lists some of the tools and approaches organizations can use to enhance their sensitivity to weak signals.[99]

Because serendipity is such a key ingredient in the stew of invention, it's essential that any process of discovery is

Fig 7-2 Improving Sense-making

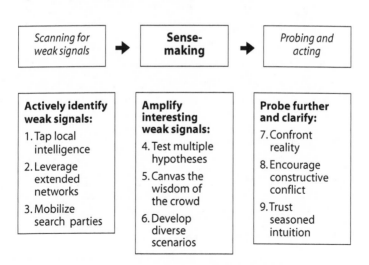

Scanning for weak signals	➡	Sense-making	➡	Probing and acting
Actively identify weak signals: 1. Tap local intelligence 2. Leverage extended networks 3. Mobilize search parties		**Amplify interesting weak signals:** 4. Test multiple hypotheses 5. Canvas the wisdom of the crowd 6. Develop diverse scenarios		**Probe further and clarify:** 7. Confront reality 8. Encourage constructive conflict 9. Trust seasoned intuition

designed in a manner that's "loose" enough to allow for random error. It can be difficult to put this principle into practice, however. Few research centers would encourage their scientists to keep labs that look like hurricane disaster areas. Even fewer would encourage their researchers to spend their spare time painting with their culture loops. Research grants—the Holy Grail, and the key measure of progress and success, in the scientific world—are rarely awarded to those who demonstrate eccentric, one-of-a-kind behavior. This raises a deeper question. Does the quest for perfection—in people's personal or professional lives—actually *reduce* the chance of brilliant discovery? I believe that it does. This is part of what drives me to theorize about, research, and write on mistakes. I don't mean mistakes that yield huge payoffs due to dumb luck, but mistakes that are stepping stones toward profound new insights.

I'll close with a story that underscores both the role of random error, as well as the value of organizational vigilance about investigating a peripheral sign.[100] Over a decade ago, the Dutch drug maker Organon was conducting clinical trials for a new antihistamine. The secretary in charge of registering the trial volunteers for their medical checkups noticed something: some members of the group were unusually cheerful and friendly. An extraneous observation, perhaps, but one she felt was worth sharing with the managers running the trial. The managers were intrigued and decided to dig deeper. To their surprise, they discovered that all of the giddy participants were in the group that was taking the drug. Ultimately, the original compound failed as envisioned: it proved unsuccessful as an allergy fighter. But by then the managers knew that they had something better on their hands: a treatment for depression. The drug was further developed and subsequently marketed as Tolvon by Organon. It turned out to be very successful. This product would never have materialized if the company had not embarked on a new compound to alleviate symptoms of allergies. Even though that pathway proved to be a mistake, it contained a silver lining that was spotted by an especially vigilant employee. This person paid close attention to details and trusted what she saw. Managers, in turn, were receptive to hearing her input and took it seriously enough to dig deeper. It takes a special organization to explore the edges this way, one involving many prepared minds that are willing to share information and explore faint stirrings at the periphery more deeply. It requires a culture of curiosity—one in which leaders encourage people at all levels to be inquisitive, observant, and nuanced in their declarations.

Epilogue
Musing About Mistakes

Even the knowledge of my own fallibility cannot keep me from making mistakes. Only when I fall do I get up again.
—VINCENT VAN GOGH [101]

The very fact that you are reading this sentence is itself a testimony to the great power of mistakes. The human species evolved through a long sequence of random errors in our DNA. Most of these errors resulted from damage to the genetic code, due to radiation, infection, pollution, and other sources of change in the DNA of all kinds of creatures. Most of these mutations led to unproductive failures, such as extinction, but occasionally there was a notable success. Natural selection then plays its part, sorting out the good mistakes from the bad or indifferent. Through this process, prehistoric reptiles managed to wriggle their way from sea to land, from slithering to crawling, and finally to walking. For humans, it led to reading and playing tennis as well as inventing new ideas and playing with microbes. The human species is especially adept at participating in the chaos and order we think of as life on the planet.

A similar process is at work in your own life. The mistakes you make are part and parcel of your life course. You might as well learn to embrace them. You will never learn more in life than you did during the skinned-knee era of early childhood, when you did not yet have an ego to protect. Once you developed a sense of self-consciousness, you came to view mistakes as unwelcome intruders, reminders of your limitations. Such humility came at a cost: you lost some of the curiosity, the impulse to learn, that governed your early years. Understanding yourself as a product of mistakes, and trying to profit from this awareness, is one step toward recovering a learning orientation, the broad-mindedness that was your birthright.

When you grow up and develop expertise, you start to devalue mistakes. You spend less time learning and more time achieving or harvesting. You become efficient and effective and embrace the goal of making fewer mistakes. As a society, we all benefit from this collective maturation. Our societal structures gain an orchestrated sense of purpose; harmful errors are reduced or eliminated. But along the path to perfection, we have, perhaps, sacrificed those special mistakes that are essential to our future learning—and even our survival. The key is to aim for, and strike, a kind of exquisite balance. This is imperative in an environment that is unstable, at times when paradigms are shifting, such as the Pearl Harbor example in the previous chapter—a moment when peacetime was being fractured by the threat of war. In these circumstances, an unwillingness to make mistakes, and a subsequent unwillingness to learn, may spell disaster.

Perhaps it is a clever evolutionary feature that makes young people reckless and prone to error. When you are inexperienced, you have little to lose, and the need for self-discovery is paramount. Mistakes are your only way to make sense of the complex, dynamic, and changing world around you. Steve Jobs, founder of Apple Computer and a maestro at the meld of technology and marketing, emphasized this point during a commencement address in June of 2005 at Stanford University.[102] Significantly, Jobs was not a Stanford graduate. He enrolled at Reed College but did not complete his degree. Here is how Jobs recounted the opportunity that arose when he dropped out and its eventual, unexpected payoff:

Reed College at that time offered perhaps the best calligraphy instruction in the country. Throughout the campus, every poster, every label on every drawer, was beautifully hand calligraphed. Because I had dropped out and didn't have to take the normal classes, I decided to take a calligraphy class to learn how to do this. I learned about serif and san serif typefaces, about varying the amount of space between different letter combinations, about what makes great typography great. It was beautiful, historical, artistically subtle in a way that science can't capture, and I found it fascinating.

None of this had even a hope of any practical application in my life. But ten years later, when we were designing the first Macintosh computer, it all came back to me. And we designed it all into the Mac. It was the first computer with beautiful typography. If I had never dropped in on that single course in college, the Mac would have never had multiple typefaces or proportionally spaced fonts. And since Windows just copied the Mac, it's likely that no personal computer would have them. If I had never dropped out, I would have never dropped in on this calligraphy class, and personal computers might not have the wonderful typography that they do. Of course it was impossible to connect the dots looking forward when I was in college. But it was very, very clear looking backwards ten years later. Again, you can't connect the dots looking forward; you can only connect them looking backwards. So you have to trust that the dots will somehow connect in your future. You have to trust in something—your gut, destiny, life, karma, whatever. This approach has never let me down, and it has made all the difference in my life.

Steve Jobs's story is an eloquent expression of one of the central premises of this book: as a young person, he trusted his intuition about what he needed enough to make bold, unconventional decisions. (Interestingly, Bill Gates, founder of Microsoft and traditionally Jobs's most powerful rival, made the same decision, dropping out of Harvard during his sophomore year.) His actions flew in the face of conventional wisdom and certainly would have been viewed, by most people, as "mistakes." But without these sequential errors, he would not have landed where he did—at the helm of one of the most innovative and well-recognized technology companies of his time.

According to the oft-cited quote by the Restoration poet Alexander Pope, "To err is human, and to forgive divine."[103] This book contends that to err can be divine as well (if you are human). Mistakes have been the cause of great discoveries and revolutionary new insights. It was *bad judgment* that led the Wright brothers to try to fly: everybody knew at the time that humans couldn't fly and never would. In 1895, just eight years before their fragile construct took to the air, Lord Kelvin, the esteemed British mathematician, physicist, and president of the British Royal Society, had unambiguously declared that "heavier-than-air flying machines are impossible."[104] It was relative ignorance that prompted Albert Einstein, a lowly patent clerk in a Swiss law office, to pose some silly questions about the nature of time, space, and energy. Had he studied a bit more physics, he would not have posed such ignorant questions. It was sloppy inattention that allowed discarded petri dishes to pile up in Fleming's laboratory in London, thereby allowing some unusual patterns of bacterial growth. Had he been tidier, he would never have discovered the miraculous healing power of penicillin, the world's most successful drug, which has saved millions of lives.

How Successful People View Mistakes

It should be clear by now that most of us need a more inviting view of mistakes. Leaders in different walks of life often remark on how mistakes that once appeared to be regrettable and painful turned out to be valuable, even brilliant. To inspire you to embrace mistakes as learning opportunities, let's examine how some very successful people reflected on their own favorite mistakes. Although these stories are anecdotal, they capture the spirit of the book. Many accomplished people have learned the hard way how to profit from mistakes. It is instructive to listen to their examples and extract some lessons.

Fortune magazine once asked business leaders to recount some of their most instructive mistakes. Jack Welch, the former CEO of General Electric and one of the most successful business leaders of his time, replied that mistakes taught him to trust his gut more.[105] This is not always easy for analytically driven engineers. When Welch was exploring buying the Wall Street firm Kidder, Peabody and Co., his intuition told him not to proceed even though his rational side propelled him to buy the company. Welch felt he picked up weak signals that the firm's leaders cared more about individual bonuses than team play, suggesting that the culture tolerated prima donnas, as long as they delivered. But he ignored these signals, as well as other soft clues, and proceeded with the acquisition. GE paid the price when Kidder, Peabody went under due to scandal and malfeasance. Leaders unavoidably will make mistakes; what matters is whether they learn and get better. To do so, you need the right attitude, and you need to embrace your mistakes. As A. G. Lafley, Procter & Gamble's outstanding and remarkably modest former CEO, put it so well, "I think of my failures as a gift."[106]

There are also many illuminating mistakes from the worlds of sports, arts, and the humanities and sciences that demonstrate how people benefit from mistakes. Consider, for example, how professional golfer J. P. Hayes managed to turn a wrong ball into the right move. Things were not going well for him in 2008: he failed to make the cut in eleven consecutive golf tournaments, lost his Professional Golf Association (PGA) playing card, and was disqualified from the second stage of qualifying school by playing a prototype type of golf ball not yet approved by the PGA. Late that night, when he realized that he had played an illegal ball, he called tour officials from his hotel room to report his mistake. No one else had noticed it; it was unlikely that anyone ever would have. Word spread of his refreshing honesty. The phone began to ring off the hook: sponsors, journalists, friends, and other players. Even the PGA honored him with unsolicited exemptions for multiple choice tournaments, including Pebble Beach.

Another golfing example further illustrates the positive side of error. If all golf players tried to master the textbook stance and swing, competition would be fierce but with little innovation. The game advances faster if some players defy the textbook swing and try something different. Luckily for golf, there are quite a few top-ranked players who never had a lesson. Gerry "Bubba" Watson, who has several PGA wins under his belt, still has not taken his first lesson. But he really does not want to: "No, sir, I never felt a need for it. I'll never take a lesson. If I start playing bad golf, I'll just have to find me a new job."[107] Other top players with hardly any lessons include Jim Furyk, who was coached only by his father, and Luke Donald. We can think of those who defy convention as social mutations, akin to genetic anomalies that have propelled the human species to where it is today.

In a fully rational world, contenders in any walk of life are well advised to emulate the world's top performers. But if many do so, this will lead, in time, to everyone following the same approach, perhaps even using the same top coaches. The end result would be that everyone plays the same style of game, with reduced variance across players. If so, there might not be much competitive distance among the top players. This happens in business as well. When too many companies compete on the same basis, copying each other's best strategies, competition heats up, profits go down, and only a few will make real money. The better strategy is to *shake up* the strategy, pursue blue rather than red oceans, and tilt the game in one's favor, since the best minds in business or sports have already squeezed most new insights from the existing model.[108] The question, of course, is how to do this. The best hope is for random error or deliberate mistakes to reveal new ways. Most of these mutations will yield nothing of value—as in biological evolution—but a few might be absolutely brilliant.

Mistakes can help science as well as sports or business. The history of science is full of wrong turns that seem necessary if one is going to stumble upon that occasional brilliant insight. Physics especially leaped ahead thanks to mistakes, starting with Isaac Newton sitting under a tree from which an apple fell on his head. Famed physicist Stephen Hawking once advanced a bold theory that black holes destroy information. This was like waving a red flag in front of his colleagues, since quantum mechanics proclaims that information can never be destroyed. Eventually, Hawking was proved wrong, but his mistaken theory opened an important new avenue of thought in physics. As theoretical physicist John Schwartz of the California Institute of Technology put it, "This is the best example of an influential wrong result." Often it is far better to be wrong and relevant in science than to be right and irrelevant. The worst putdown in science is that which the Nobel laureate physicist Wolfgang Pauli inflicted upon a banal theory: he complained, "It isn't even wrong."[109]

Courting Error and Mistake

The examples in this epilogue are mostly about remarkable individuals who learned from mistakes that occurred at random. I cite them because they illustrate that success is enhanced if mistakes are viewed as gifts. The deeper lesson in our book is that it often pays to *design* for these gifts of learning rather than waiting for them to occur by accident. This deliberate approach to making mistakes—in order to accelerate learning or achieve higher performance—plays a crucial role in music, especially jazz. When trumpet great Wynton Marsalis was asked during a goodwill music tour to Cuba how important and valuable mistakes are, he replied, "Very important, because if you're not making mistakes, you're not trying. That is the art of jazz. It's an art of negotiation, of communication."[110] As one guide to jazz improvisation explains, "We must accept each idea that we present to the group as valid. If each idea that is presented is utilized in some way by that individual, the other people in the group can respond knowing full well that it will be included to some degree. One can say that no idea that is presented is faulty. There is no such thing as a mistake but only opportunity to explore a path that may not have been considered. Each idea presented can be used in a positive way."[111]

Jazz great Miles Davis would have agreed. He urged his followers "not to fear mistakes—there are none." Even classical music giants resonate to this theme. Russian composer Igor Stravinsky (1882–1971) said, "I have learned throughout my life as a composer chiefly through mistakes and pursuits of false assumptions, not my exposure to founts of wisdom and knowledge."[112]

Artists are especially adept at struggling with deliberate mistakes. Their very willingness to enter a field as uncertain and unstable as art means that they are, by nature, far less risk-averse than the rest of us. Artists are willing to live at the edge, embrace deviance, and challenge bourgeois conventions. They accept that mistakes are vital as well as rather uncomfortable companions along the road to success. For most artists, there is far more failure than success at first, a necessary condition, it seems, if one is to have a decent chance of achieving something of note. The phenomenally successful British novelist J. K. Rowling emphasized this key point during her commencement address at Harvard in 2008. She explained how mistakes and failures had taken her to a point of deep insight about herself, prior to her smashing success with the Harry Potter series:

> *By any conventional measure, a mere seven years after my graduation day, I had failed on an epic scale. An exceptionally short-lived marriage had imploded, and I was jobless, a lone parent and as poor as it is possible to be in modern Britain without being homeless. The fears my parents had had for me, and that I had had for myself, had both come to pass, and by every usual standard, I was the biggest failure I knew. Why do I talk about the benefits of failure?—simply because failure meant a stripping away of the inessential. I stopped pretending to myself that I was anything other than what I was, and began to direct all my energy into finishing the only work that mattered to me. Had I really succeeded at anything else, I might never have found the determination to succeed in the one arena I believed I truly belonged. I was set free, because my greatest fear had already been realized, and I was still alive, and I still had a daughter whom I adored, and I had an old typewriter and a big idea. And so rock bottom became the solid foundation on which I rebuilt my life.*

Besides being good at defying convention, hitting rock bottom, and then rising to new creative heights, some artists are skilled at incorporating random errors into their creative process as well. Jackson Pollock, in a well-known example, created his famous "drip technique" of painting because his constrained financial circumstances required him to use resin-based household paints, which were thinner and more liquid than the more expensive artist's paints. In his path-breaking 1922 novel *Ulysses*, Joyce comments that "a man of genius makes no mistakes. His errors are volitional and are the portals of discovery."[113] There is an intriguing story about Joyce when he was writing *Finnegans Wake*. At this point in his career, he was nearly blind, and so he composed by dictating to a secretary (playwright Samuel Beckett, no less). The narration is stream-of-consciousness. During this dictation, there was a knock at the door. Joyce went to the door and had a conversation with his visitor in the doorway. Meanwhile, Beckett furiously transcribed every word. After Joyce returned, he asked Beckett to read back the last section of the work, and Beckett included the conversation at the door, expecting that the master would instruct him to strike it. Instead, Joyce told him to leave it in—it is part of the text of the published story. It was, perhaps, to use Joyce's own term, a portal of discovery.

In Conclusion

The deeper theme of this book is the role of surprise in our lives, whether in the form of mistakes or good luck. I chose to hone in on negative surprises because these are, by definition, more difficult to embrace and accept. It is easy to dwell on a positive surprise, where the outcome exceeds our expectations. We recount our good fortune to others, debate why it happened, and dream happy thoughts about Lady Fortune smiling on us. Negative surprises, such as outright failures or embarrassing setbacks, seldom enjoy such special attention. We want to forget about them as soon as possible and are unlikely to share them with a large audience.

This reaction is human but also misguided. The deepest lessons reside at the far side of failure. If you want to learn, it is better to be enormously wrong than a little wrong, since the large mistakes form the most vivid markers of where your assumptions, mental model, or approach are flawed. In other words, fail big—and thereby learn to dwell on the far side of failure, overcoming your emotional obstacles to learning.

A good starting point is learning to laugh at your own mistakes. This is what successful people often do especially well. Don't take yourself too seriously. The obituary of Fritz Bach, a pioneer in reducing the risks of heart transplant rejection in humans, cites his many scientific accomplishments.[114] I had the pleasure of meeting Dr. Bach on several occasions and was struck by his modesty and deep humanity. The obituary concluded, touchingly, with a comment that Dr. Bach most enjoyed an early photo of himself in which he is shown giving a lecture about a new genetic theory of his that proved to be completely wrong.

The great virtue of mistakes, whether they occur accidentally or by design, is their ability to enlarge our range of experience, shrink our ego, and thereby increase the chance of discovery. If you accept that humans are myopic and largely unaware of their own bounded rationality, then some degree of mistake-making is appropriate and welcome. This is especially hard in organizations, but leaders can start by instituting awards like the Golden Egg.[115] The president of an Ann Arbor business concocted this to make sure his organization would extract as much learning as possible from past failures. He views mistakes as valuable assets the company had paid for but not fully harvested yet. So, he asked managers to share their mistakes at their monthly meeting, akin to the mortality and morbidity meetings at hospitals, when medical errors are reviewed. At first there was reluctance to open up, but eventually these confessionals became a favorite part of the session. The president decided to give a symbolic award to managers who had egg on their face and were courageous enough to share the learning. He devised a simple and modest trophy—a L'eggs pantyhose plastic egg with some gold spray paint—that signified the best mistake of the month.

At first, the trophies stayed in the desk drawer of the (un)lucky winner. But over time, winners became proud enough to place the trophy on their desk. This naturally prompted conversations with visitors about how managers were able to convert egg on their face into delicious omelets rich with insight and learning. In short, the company president managed to change the organizational culture from hiding mistakes to celebrating them and sharing the learning.

To fully harness the benefits of mistakes, organizations must consciously design failure into their strategies. New portals of discovery will open and innovation will spark. The notion of deliberate mistakes is a powerful but much under-utilized strategy to help organizations accelerate their learning and achieve success. It should be part of any strategy, plan, and performance review. The key question companies need to address is not "*Should* we make mistakes?" but rather, "*Which* mistakes should we make in order to test our deeply held assumptions?"

It is my fondest hope that this book has altered your view of mistakes and failure. I believe that we should view certain mistakes as gifts. If you are bold enough to embrace this mind-set, it will profoundly change the way you approach your work, family, and indeed your life. It will alter where you look for success and how you respond to unexpected, unfortunate outcomes. You will become more tolerant of imperfection, extract more benefit from human error, and live your life with less unhealthy regret. Embrace and champion this counterintuitive strategy! The reward will be new insights, new power, and new discoveries.

Appendix A
Einstein's 23 Mistakes

1. 1905: Mistake in clock synchronization procedure on which Einstein based special relativity
2. 1905: Failure to consider Michelson-Morley experiment
3. 1905: Mistake in transverse mass of high-speed particles
4. 1905: Multiple mistakes in the mathematics and physics used in calculation of viscosity of liquids, from which Einstein deduced the size of molecules
5. 1905: Mistakes in the relationship between thermal radiation and quanta of light
6. 1905: Mistake in the first proof of $E = mc^2$
7. 1906: Mistakes in the second, third, and fourth proofs of $E = mc^2$
8. 1907: Mistake in the synchronization procedure for accelerated clocks
9. 1907: Mistakes in the Principle of Equivalence of gravitation and acceleration
10. 1911: Mistake in the first calculation of the bending of light
11. 1913: Mistake in the first attempt at a theory of general relativity
12. 1914: Mistake in the fifth proof of $E = mc^2$
13. 1915: Mistake in the Einstein-de Haas experiment
14. 1915: Mistakes in several attempts at theories of general relativity
15. 1916: Mistake in the interpretation of Mach's principle
16. 1917: Mistake in the introduction of the cosmological constant (the "biggest blunder," in Einstein's own words)

17. 1919: Mistakes in two attempts to modify general relativity
18. 1925: Mistakes and more mistakes in the attempts to formulate a unified theory
19. 1927: Mistakes in discussions with Bohr on quantum uncertainties
20. 1933: Mistakes in interpretation of quantum mechanics (does God play dice?)
21. 1934: Mistake in the sixth proof of $E = mc^2$
22. 1939: Mistake in the interpretation of the Schwarzschild singularity and gravitational collapse (the "black hole")
23. 1946: Mistake in the seventh proof of $E = mc^2$

Appendix B
Expected Utility Analysis

Expected utility theory is the standard economic model for defining rational decision making. It is based on various axioms that define rational behavior; then, some key theorems are derived to prove that maximizing expected utility is the optimal course of action for a decision maker who wishes to abide by these axioms.[116]

Let's illustrate the basic idea of this theory using a simple example. Suppose a senior in high school has to decide which college to attend after having been accepted at five schools. The first step in expected utility analysis would be to systematically list the pros and cons of each school. Then the student would have to think deeply about key trade-offs, such as tuition cost versus the quality of the school, proximity to home versus exposure to new experiences, or, say, academic challenge versus time for social activities. Next, the student would link the pros and cons of each school to these personal values in order to produce a preliminary ranking. If the schools at the top of this ranking are close, we would recommend getting more information or perhaps ask the student to rethink the trade-offs or other subjective input. Once all relevant information is in hand, we are ready to perform a systematic analysis in which we measure the utility of each option and then weigh it by the probability of achieving it.

To keep this illustration simple, suppose the student is left with just two top schools to choose between. To simplify further, assume that all relevant considerations have been mapped into a single overall attractiveness measure, called utility. Since there is uncertainty about how much utility either school will actually yield after four years, let's express these risks in terms of three levels of utility (High, Medium, and Low), with subjective probabilities attached. Suppose school A entails the following risk profile [45%, H; 30%, M; 25%, L]. This means that there is 45% chance that the experience of attending school A will at the end of four years be judged as High in satisfaction, a 30% chance of its scoring Medium, and a 25% of scoring Low. The probabilities in this example are subjective, supplied by the decision maker or their advisers. Suppose we now assign the following subjective utility values: H = 10, M = 5, and L = 0. We can then compute the expected utility score for school A as being: .45*10 + .3*5 and .25*0 = 6. Next, assume that school B has a somewhat different risk profile, namely: [60%, H; 10%, M; 30%, L]. Which school is better for our student? To find out, we need to calculate the expected utility of B as well, which would be .6*10 + .1*5 + .3*0 = .65. According to this analysis, the student should enroll in school B, since it has the highest expected utility.

Appendix C
Portfolio Justifications

The portfolio argument in support of deliberate mistakes can be made at the individual as well as the market level. The field of finance first solved the problem of optimal portfolio balance for an investor operating in isolation and then extended it to market-based investments. Let's examine each in the context of deliberate mistakes, which we define as tests or experiments offering a negative expected return. A risk-averse investor would never wish to invest any money in such projects when viewed in isolation. But if these investments exhibit inverse correlations with other assets, it might nonetheless pay to do so.

Harry Markowitz solved the complex problem of how to allocate a fixed investment amount across many securities when all that is known are the mean, variance, and correlations for each.[117] For mathematical ease, Markowitz assumed normal distributions of returns and measured the investor's degree of risk aversion just in terms of mean-variance trade-offs. Suppose a risk investor used this basic model to optimally allocate $1 million across n different investments. Next, the investor is given the opportunity to reallocate some of these funds to a new investment. Should any funds be invested in this $(n+1)$ security if it offers a negative expected return and exhibits strong inverse covariances with all other investments? The answer is usually yes: a risk-averse investor should be willing to sacrifice some expected return so as to lower the overall risk (measured as variance) of the portfolio.

This pathbreaking work subsequently spawned the development of the capital asset pricing model (CAPM) in finance, for which Harry Markowitz, Merton Miller, and William Sharpe were awarded the Nobel Prize in Economics.[118] The CAPM examines how rational investors should behave when operating in an efficient market where they can borrow money and/or invest in a risk-free asset. The original CAPM model showed that (1) capital markets would only pay an extra return for systematic risk (measured as beta) and (2) each investor should hold a portfolio comprised of just the risk-free asset and the market portfolio.[119] This market-based model further supports the notion that investing in a negative return option can be rational. Suppose a particular asset has a negative covariance with other assets, so it will have a negative beta. Let's say its beta is -0.75, which means that this security dampens the effect of the market and will usually move in a direction opposite to that of the market. Let's further assume that the risk-free rate is 4%, and the market risk premium is 7%. In that case, the required return = (-.75 x 7%) + 4% = −1.25%. This negative number implies that investors would be willing to accept a security offering an expected return of −1.25% (that is, a loss on average) in order to dampen their overall portfolio risk. This simple numerical CAPM example supports the idea of making deliberate mistakes using a traditional framework of economic rationality.

In sum, a portfolio case can be made at times for investing in projects that are expected to yield a negative return, at both the individual and the corporate level. For a risk-averse decision maker, it may be worth putting some money in a project expected to yield a loss, provided this investment offers a sufficient hedge in case other investments sour. Even though that seemingly inferior project will not raise profit expectations, it can help reduce losses in case bad scenarios happen.

Similarly, a deliberate mistake can be viewed as a hedge against conventional wisdom, one that will have a high payoff when the majority view happens to be wrong (but a loss otherwise, in all likelihood).

Appendix D
How Your Mind Plays Tricks

The following terms, from the field of cognitive psychology, all refer to "tricks" your mind plays. Most of these mechanisms—filtering, distorted inference, and bolstering—allow you to cling tenaciously to your dominant frame of mind. Recognizing your own proclivity to fall into these traps is one way to assure a more open, inquiring mind.

Filtering

As noted with the wrong cards, what we actually pay attention to is very much determined by what we expect to see. Psychologists call this selective perception. If something doesn't fit, we often distort reality to make it fit our mental model rather than challenging our fundamental assumptions. A related phenomenon is suppression, or the refusal to acknowledge an unpleasant reality because it is too discordant. The extreme example is that of an ostrich burying its head in the sand upon seeing danger and believing that this will make the threat disappear.

Distorted Inference

Whatever information passes through our cognitive and emotional filters may be subject to further distortion. One well-known bias is rationalization: interpreting evidence in a way that sustains a desired belief. We fall victim to this, for example, when trying to shift blame for a mistake we made to someone else or to external circumstances. Wishful thinking leads us to see the world only in a pleasing way, denying subtle evidence that a child is abusing drugs or that a spouse is being unfaithful. Another common interpretation bias is egocentrism, according to which we overemphasize our own role in the events we seek to explain. This self-aggrandizement is related to the fundamental attribution bias that causes us to ascribe more importance to our own actions than to those of others. For example, managers may view their organization as being a more central actor than it really is.

Bolstering

Not only do we filter the limited information that reaches us, but we then tend to bolster our case by searching for evidence that supports our view. To achieve that, we might disproportionately talk to people who already agree with us. This insidious confirmation bias causes us to discount evidence that is contrary to our viewpoint. Over time, our opinions become frozen and our attitudes hardened as we immunize ourselves from contradictory evidence. Indeed, we may even engage in selective memory and forget those inconvenient facts that don't fit the overall picture. The hindsight bias similarly distorts our memories such that our original doubts get erased. Thus a vicious circle is created in which we exacerbate the earlier biases and get trapped in a self-sealing echo chamber.

Acknowledgments

As noted in the memorial dedication up front, I owe a large measure of debt to Robert E. Gunther, with whom I developed a book proposal on brilliant mistakes several years ago. In those early days, Robert and I received valuable editorial guidance and encouragement from Jill Marsal as our literary agent. Following Robert's tragic and untimely death in 2009, I received full cooperation from his wife, Cindie Wisting Gunther, as I tried to relaunch the book project in a somewhat different direction. Toward the end of the writing stage, I benefited greatly from excellent editing by Gretchen Anderson who kindly served as a much needed "ruthless editor" (her words). Gretchen painstakingly reworked every chapter and made sure the book's flow captured the gist of my viewpoints in an accessible manner. I am also grateful for the constructive feedback of my wife, Joyce, and daughter, Kim, both of whom read multiple versions and helped improve the draft each time.

As the manuscript evolved, I received valuable feedback from Russell Ackoff, Jackie Gnepp, Robin Hogarth, Josh Klayman, J. Edward Russo, Jeremy Schoemaker, Alan Shapiro, Scott Snyder, and Anthonie Zoomers. Josh Klayman especially focused on the deeper underpinnings of the book, emphasizing that mistakes constitute a special class of surprises. My cousin Jeremy Schoemaker took a deep dive into the manuscript while Hurricane Irene battered Princeton, New Jersey, and offered insightful comments on many chapters. Various colleagues at our company Decision Strategies International (*www.decisionstrat.com*) also were kind enough to review earlier drafts, including Guy Davis, Rob-Jan de Jong, Eric Lerch, Viraj Narayanan, Roch Parayre, Camelia Ram, Jarrad Roeder, Franklin Shen, Eric Strang, and Aghogho Ughwanogho. Their comments highlighted practical as well as conceptual points, and I am grateful for their suggestions about how to apply the book's insight in business.

Last, but not least, I received excellent feedback and support from Wharton Professor Steve Kobrin and Shannon Berning while both were in the midst of launching Wharton Digital Press. They went far beyond their roles as publisher and executive editor, respectively, and helped me shape the manuscript from a rough draft into a more cogent and polished work. They recognized promising avenues and flagged unnecessary detours as various drafts landed on their desks. In each instance, their advice was insightful, constructive, and practical, keeping the target audience in mind all along. I thank all of the above for their generous help while holding no one responsible for any blemishes or defects that remain.

Notes

1 James Joyce, *Ulysses* (New York: Vintage, 1990).

2 For additional engineering examples of learning by mistake, from bridges to optical projection, see Henry Petroski, *Success Through Failure: The Paradox of Design* (Princeton, NJ: Princeton University Press, 2008).

3 Albert Einstein, "On the Electrodynamics of Moving Bodies," *Annalen der Physik* 17 (1905): 891–921.This was one of four brilliant papers Einstein published in this annus mirabilis; see *http://en.wikipedia.org/wiki/Annus_Mirabilis_papers.*

4 Hans Ohanian, *Einstein's Mistakes: The Human Failings of Genius* (New York: W. W. Norton, 2008).

5 The basic idea behind a Six Sigma program is to reduce variance so that manufacturing or service defects occur less, until ultimately their frequency falls in the far tail of the probability distribution, six standard deviations (or sigmas) away from the mean. This is great if you want consistency but may hamper innovation, since creativity feeds on outliers; see *http://www.businessweek.com/magazine/content/07_24/b4038406.htm.*

6 The field of behavioral economics was largely in its infancy and decision psychology was just emerging. Merton Miller, a pioneer of efficient market research, deemed behavioral decision research to be a mistake, a blind alley. Other leading Chicago economists, including George Stigler, Gene Fama, and Gary Becker, shared the sentiment. I had the pleasure of debating these matters with them. My critique of the rational model can be found in P. J. H. Schoemaker, "The Expected Utility Model: Its Variants, Purposes, Evidence and Limitations," *Journal of Economic Literature* 20 (June 1982): 529–63.

7 For example, Herbert Simon was an earlier behavioral researcher who received the Nobel Prize in Economics in 1978 for pathbreaking work on decision making, organization theory, computer science, and artificial intelligence.

8 *http://www.sjdm.org/*; John Baron was kind enough to supply information on membership size.

[9] Steven D. Levitt and Stephen J. Dubner, *Freakonomics: A Rogue Economist Explores the Hidden Side of Everything* (New York: HarperCollins, 2005); Dan Ariely, *Predictably Irrational* (New York: HarperCollins, 2008); Richard H. Thaler and Cass R. Sunstein, *Nudge* (New Haven, CT: Yale University Press, 2007).

[10] Cass Sunstein serves as the administrator of the White House Office of Information and Regulatory Affairs in the Obama administration. Richard Thaler has been an adviser to President Obama and his administration.

[11] The Beatles quotes are drawn from Mark Lewisohn, *The Complete Beatles Chronicle* (London: Hamlyn, 2000).

[12] When the Beatles released "I Want to Hold Your Hand," on December 26, 1963, the number 1 record on the U.S. Hit Parade was Sister Sourire's "Dominique."

[13] Bill Harry, *The Beatles Encyclopedia*, rev. ed. (London: Virgin Publishing, 2001), 375.

[14] Alan Mackay, ed., *The Harvest of a Quiet Eye: a Selection of Scientific Quotations* (London: Taylor & Francis, 1977).

[15] See *http://www.utas.edu.au/docs/humsoc/kierkegaard/resources/Kierkquotes.html.*

[16] Baruch Fischhoff and Ruth Beyth, "'I Knew It Would Happen'—Remembered Probabilities of Once-Future Things," *Organizational Behavior and Human Performance* 13 (1975):1–16. For causes of hindsight bias, see Terry Connolly and Edward W. Bukszar, "Hindsight Bias: Self-Flattery or Cognitive Error?" *Journal of Behavioral Decision Making* 3 (1990): 205–11.

[17] See *http://www.merriam-webster.com/dictionary/mistake?show=1&t=1315568847.*

[18] The need to feel in control is discussed in Ellen Langer, "The Illusion of Control," *Journal of Personality and Social Psychology* 32 (1975): 322–28. Shelley E. Taylor and Jonathon D. Brown offer an interesting perspective on the positive value of illusions in "Illusion and Well-Being: A Social Psychological Perspective on Mental Health," *Psychological Bulletin* 193, no. 2 (1988): 193–210. The relationships between the illusion of control, wishful thinking, and optimism are subtle, as examined in David V. Budescu and Meira Bruderman, "The Relationship Between the Illusion of Control and the Desirability Bias," *Journal of Behavioral Decision Making* 8 (1995): 109–25.

[19] Richard Kradin, *The Placebo Response and the Power of Unconscious Healing* (London: Routledge, 2008).

[20] See *http://www.enotes.com/biz-encyclopedia/hawthorne-experiments.*

[21] Robert Frost, *Mountain Interval.* Quinn & Boden Company (1916).

22 *The Speaker's Electronic Reference Collection*, AApex Software, 1994.

23 In general, acts of omission (not choosing or acting) are safer than acts of commission; see Jonathan Baron and Ilana Ritov, "Reference Points and Omission Bias," *Organizational Behavior and Human Decision Processes* 59, no. 3 (September 1994): 475–98).

24 See *http://www.biographybase.com/biography/Fish_Stanley.html*.

25 See *http://thinkexist.com/quotes/soichiro_honda/*.

26 See *http://www.medleague.com/Articles/president/topquotes.htm*; *http://www.edisonmuckers.org/thomas-edison-lightbulb/*.

27 Chuck Salter, "Failure Doesn't Suck," *Fast Company*, May 2007, 44.

28 Paul F. Lazarsfeld, "The American Soldier: An Expository Review," *Public Opinion Quarterly* 13 (1949): 377–404.

29 Scott O. Lilienfeld, Steven Jay Lynn, John Ruscio, and Barry L. Beyerstein, *50 Great Myths of Popular Psychology: Shattering Widespread Misconceptions about Human Behavior* (Hoboken, NJ: Wiley-Blackwell, 2009).

30 G. J. S. Wilde, "Critical Issues in Risk Homeostatis Theory," *Risk Analysis* 2, no. 4 (1982): 249–58.

31 These three examples are discussed further in Fortune's "101 Dumbest Moments in Business in 2007"; for all of them, see *http://money.cnn.com/galleries/2007/fortune/0712/gallery.101_dum best.fortune/index.html*.

32 Jena McGregor, "How Failure Breeds Success," *BusinessWeek*, July 10, 2006, pp. 42-52.

33 Obituary of John R. Stallings Jr., *New York Times*, January 19, 2009.

34 See *http://www.innocenceproject.org/Content/162.php*.

35 See *http://select.nytimes.com/2007/07/23/us/23bar.html?_r=1&oref =slogin*.

36 Gary L. Wells and Elizabeth F. Loftus, eds., *Eyewitness Testimony: Psychological Perspectives* (New York: Cambridge University Press, 1984). See also Eugene Winograd, "What You Should Know About Eyewitness Testimony," *Contemporary Psychology* 31, no. 5 (1986): 332–34.

37 The classic reference on groupthink is Irving Janis, *Groupthink: Psychological Studies of Policy Decisions and Fiascos*, 2nd ed. (New York: Houghton Mifflin, 1982). For a critical review of groupthink as a psychological model, see Won-Woo Park, "A Review of Research on Groupthink," *Journal of Behavioral Decision Making* 3, no. 4 (October–December 1990): 229–46.

38 There are many other such examples, including the alleged sexual abuse of autistic children in the infamous Salem trials. Parents and teachers were accused, vilified, and arrested by an overly zealous prosecutor. Child experts obtained incriminating testimony that was inadvertently fed to the autistic children via a new communication technique; see Stephen J. Ceci and Maggie Bruck,

"Suggestibility of the Child Witness: A Historical Review and Synthesis," *Psychological Bulletin* 113, no. 3 (May 1993): 403–39.

[39] Kathryn Schulz, *Being Wrong: Adventures in the Margin of Error* (London: Portobello Books, 2010).

[40] Leon Festinger, *Theory of Cognitive Dissonance* (Palo Alto, CA: Stanford University Press, 1957).

[41] Stanly Cohen, *States of Denial: Knowing about Atrocities and Suffering* (Cambridge, UK: Polity, 2001).

[42] Jonah Lehrer, "Accept Defeat: The Neuroscience of Screwing Up," *Wired Magazine*, Dec 21, 2009; Constance Holden, "Gene Variant May Influence How People Learn from Mistakes," *Science*, Vol. 318, Dec 7, 2007, p 1539; Markus Ulsperger, "Minding Mistakes: How the Brain Monitors Errors and Learns from Goofs," *Scientific American*, August 13, 2008.

[43] Thomas S. Kuhn, *The Structure of Scientific Revolutions*, 3rd ed. (Chicago: University of Chicago Press, 1996).

[44] Daniel Kahneman, Paul Slovic, and Amos Tversky, eds., *Judgment under Uncertainty Heuristics and Biases* (New York: Cambridge University Press, 1982).

[45] J. Edward Russo and Paul J. H. Schoemaker, *Winning Decisions: Getting It Right the First Time* (New York: Doubleday, 2001).

[46] The ERIC case is described in Howard Kunreuther and Paul Freeman, *Managing Environmental Risk through Insurance* (Dordrecht, Netherlands: Kluwer Academic Publisher, 1997).

[47] J. E. Russo and P. J. H. Schoemaker, "Managing Overconfidence," *Sloan Management Review*, Winter 1992, 7–18.

[48] Alan M. Kantrow, *The Constraints of Corporate Tradition* (New York: Harper & Row, 1987).

[49] See *http://www.famous-proverbs.com/Santayana_Quotes_2.htm.*

[50] The classic paper on ambiguity is Daniel Ellsberg, "Risk, Ambiguity, and the Savage Axioms," *Quarterly Journal of Economics* 75 (1961): 643–69. Decisions with unknown probabilities have been studied by many, including H. Einhorn and R. Hogarth, "Decision Making Under Ambiguity," *Journal of Business* 59, no. 4, pt. 2 (1986): S225–55; M. Cohen, J. Jaffray, and T. Said, "Individual Behavior Under Risk and Under Uncertainty: An Experimental Study," *Theory and Decisions* 18 (1985): 203–28; Paul J. H. Schoemaker, "Choices Involving Uncertain Probabilities: Tests of Generalized Utility Models," *Journal of Economic and Organizational Behavior* 16 (1991): 295–317.

[51] Robin M. Hogarth, *Educating Intuition* (Chicago: University Of Chicago Press, 2001); Gary Klein, *The Power of Intuition: How to Use Your Gut Feelings to Make Better Decisions at Work* (New York: Doubleday, 2004). A popular book on intuition, Malcolm Gladwell, *Blink: The Power of Thinking without Thinking* (New York: Little,

Brown, 2005). For a critical review of this work, see R. S. Hogarth and P. J. H. Schoemaker, "Beyond Blink: A Challenge to Behavioral Decision Making," *Journal of Behavioral Decision Making* 18 (2005): 309–18.

[52] Groups will often end up more extreme in their judgment than the prior opinions of the group members would lead one to expect (known as polarization), provided there is a majority leaning to begin with. When two roughly equal factions exist, the group may actually moderate extreme views and end up in a less extreme position. At other times, groups may fail to think critically, as in the well-known Abilene paradox: see Kathleen M. Eisenhardt, Jean L. Kahwajy, and L. J. Bourgeois III, "Conflict and Strategic Choice: How Top Management Teams Disagree," *California Management Review* 39, no. 2 (Winter 1997).

[53] The US Marine Corps is well known for its excellent training in how to learn from mistakes. For a firsthand account, see Nathaniel C. Fick, *One Bullet Away: The Making of a Marine Officer* (Boston, MA: Houghton-Mifflin, 2005).

[54] Robert Rosenthal and Lenore Jacobson, *Pygmalion in the Classroom: Teacher Expectation and Pupils' Intellectual Development* (New York: Crown, 2003).

[55] Oscar Wilde, *Lady Windermere's Fan* (Play, 1892); see *http://search.barnesandnoble.com/Lady-Windermeres-Fan/Oscar-Wilde/p/9781420925937*; eBook, September 13, 2011 Filiquarian Publishing.

[56] These insights were presented by Jesse Treu at a management conference at the Wharton School on portfolio strategies, held in Philadelphia on November 12, 2010, and organized by the Mack Center for Technological Innovation.

[57] See *http://www.answers.com/topic/helmuth-graf-von-moltke*.

[58] See *http://en.wikipedia.org/wiki/Thomas_J._Watson*.

[59] Maria Dahvana Headley, *The Year of Yes* (New York: Hyperion, 2007).

[60] See *http://www.quotationspage.com/quote/29729.html*.

[61] The literature on overconfidence is extensive. An excellent discussion can be found in Joshua Klayman, Jack-B Soll, Claudia Gonzalez-Vallejo, and Sema Barlas, "Overconfidence: It Depends on How, What, and Whom You Ask," *Organizational Behavior and Human Decision Processes* 79, no. 3 (September 1999), 216–47.

[62] Robert Rosenthal and Kermit L. Fode, "The Effect of Experimenter Bias on the Performance of the Albino Rat," *Behavioral Science* 8, no. 3 (1963): 183–89.

[63] Robin M. Hogarth and Emre Soyer, "Sequentially Simulated Outcomes: Kind Experience versus Nontransparent Description," *Journal of Experimental Psychology* 140, no. 3 (August 2011): 434–63.

64 Karl Popper, *The Logic of Scientific Discovery*, 2nd ed. (London: Routledge, 2002). Popper's analysis of the logical asymmetry between verification and falsifiability lies at the heart of his philosophy of science.

65 For the original 2-4-6 experiment, see P. C. Wason, "On the Failure to Eliminate Hypotheses in a Conceptual Task," *Quarterly Journal of Experimental Psychology* 12 (1960): 129–40; further discussion can be found in Jonathan Baron, *Thinking and Deciding*, 3rd ed. (New York: Cambridge University Press, 2000).

66 A penetrating analysis of the bias toward confirming evidence has been presented by Joshua Klayman and Young-Won Ha, "Confirmation, Disconfirmation and Information in Hypothesis Testing," *Psychological Review* 94, no. 2 (1987): 211–28. Klayman and Ha argue that whether disconfirmation or confirmation is most suitable depends in complex ways on the kind of task one faces; see also Joshua Klayman, "Varieties of Confirmation Bias," in *Decision Making from a Cognitive Perspective*, edited by Jerome Busemeyer, Reid Hastie, and Douglas L. Medin (New York: Academic Press [Psychology of Learning and Motivation, vol. 32], 1995), 365–418.

67 "Thomas J. Watson Sr.," *The Manager's Book of Quotations*, edited by Lewis D. Eigen and Jonathan P. Siegel.

68 C. F. Hathaway Company made uniform shirts for Union soldiers during the American Civil War. It became famous for its "man with an eye patch" advertising campaign, created by Ogilvy & Mather in 1951. For more on David Ogilvy's approach to advertising, see his autobiography *Ogilvy on Advertising* (Vintage Books, 1985) or his earlier book *Confessions of an Advertising Man* (Ballantine Books, 1963).

69 Based on an interview by Michael Schrage (*schrage@media.mit.edu*), codirector of the MIT Media Lab's e-Markets Initiative; see also Daniel Kahneman, *Thinking, Fast and Slow* (Farrar, Straus, and Giroux, 2011).

70 Philosophically inclined readers will note an infinite regress problem lurking here, since I define a deliberate mistake as an action that is unwise at dominant thinking level n but smart at a higher level n+1. I will leave it to cognitive psychologists to figure out how many thinking levels there really are, but the answer seems to be at least two.

71 These methods, as well as the others in figure 5-1, are explained in the appendix of my book *Profiting from Uncertainty* (New York: Free Press, 2001); see also Hugh Courtney, *20:20 Foresight: Crafting Strategy in an Uncertain World* (Cambridge, MA: Harvard Business School Press, 2001).

[72] Avinash K. Dixit and R. S. Pindyck, "The Options Approach to Capital Investment," *Harvard Business Review*, May–June 1995, 105–15; Ian C. MacMillan and Rita Gunther McGrath, "Crafting R&D Project Portfolios," *Research Technology Management*, September–October 2002, 48–59.

[73] Larry Huston and Nabil Sakkab, "Connect and Develop: Inside Procter & Gamble's New Model for Innovation," *Harvard Business Review*, March 2006, 58–66.

[74] Rita Gunther McGrath and Ian C. MacMillan, "Discovery Driven Planning," *Harvard Business Review* (July 1995); see also Andrew Lainsbury, *Once Upon an American Dream: The Story of Euro Disneyland* (Lawrence, KS: University Press of Kansas, 2000).

[75] Clayton Christensen, *The Innovator's Dilemma* (Boston: Harvard Business School Press, 1997).

[76] The term "skunk works" is widely used in business and technical fields to describe a project or group within an organization given a high degree of autonomy, unhampered by bureaucracy, while tasked with working on advanced or secret projects; see *http://en.wikipedia.org/wiki/Skunk_Works*.

[77] Alina Tugend, *Better by Mistake: The Unexpected Benefits of Being Wrong* (New York: Riverhead, 2011).

[78] "Sci-fi Writers Join War on Terror," *USA Today*, May 30, 2007; a similar imagination approach, using fantasy documents, is advocated for organizations and government in Lee Clarke's book, *Mission Improbable: Using Fantasy Documents to Tame Disasters*, (Chicago, IL: University of Chicago Press, 1992).

[79] See *http://www.special-dictionary.com/proverbs/keywords/depth/*.

[80] Amos Tversky and Daniel Kahneman, "The Framing of Decisions and the Psychology of Choice," *Science* 211 (1981): 453-458).

[81] See *http://www.defcon.org/*.

[82] Donald F. Klein, "The Loss of Serendipity in Psychopharmacology," *Journal of the American Medical Association*, March 5, 2008, Vol. 299, No. 9, pp. 1063-1065.

[83] George Day, "Is It Real? Can We Win? Is It Worth Doing? Managing Risk and Reward in an Innovation Portfolio," *Harvard Business Review*, December 2007.

[84] John Morgan and Richard Wang, "Tournaments for Ideas," *California Management Review* 52, no. 2 (Winter 2010): 77–97.

[85] Christian Terwiesch and Karl Ulrich, *Innovation Tournaments: Creating and Selecting Exceptional Opportunities* (Cambridge, MA: Harvard Business School Press, 2009).

[86] See *http://www.nndb.com/people/348/000129958/*.

[87] See *http://www.brainyquote.com/quotes/quotes/l/louispaste134068.html*.

[88] Arthur Koestler, *Janus: A Summing Up* (New York: Random House, 1978); James L. Adams, *Conceptual Blockbusting* (Reading, MA:

Addison Wesley Longman, 1986); Edward de Bono, *Lateral Thinking: Creativity Step by Step* (New York: Harper & Row, 1973); Robert Lawrence Kuhn, ed., *Handbook for Creative and Innovative Managers* (New York: McGraw-Hill, 1987); Jane Henry, ed., *Creative Management* (Thousand Oaks, CA: Sage Publications, 1991).

[89] W. H. Hughes, *Alexander Fleming and Penicillin* (London: Priority, 1974).

[90] Robert S. Root-Bernstein, "How Scientists Really Think," *Perspectives in Biology and Medicine* 32, no. 4 (Summer 1989): 472–488.

[91] Ibid.

[92] Other well-known medical examples include the serendipitous finding that cow pox infection can offer immunity for smallpox, that lime juices can treat scurvy, or the discovery of vitamin B_{12} due to liver treatment of anemia.

[93] George S. Day and Paul J. H. Schoemaker, *Peripheral Vision: Detecting the Weak Signals That Will Make or Break Your Company* (Cambridge, MA: Harvard Business School Press, 2006).

[94] Roberta Wohlstetter, *Pearl Harbor: Warning and Decisions* (Stanford, CA: Stanford University Press, 1962); Gordon Prang, *At Dawn We Slept* (New York: Penguin Books, 1981).

[95] More specifically, Kant said that perception without conception is blind; while conception without perception is empty; see *http://www.bartleby.com/60/144.html*.

[96] Jerome S. Bruner and Leo Postman, "On the Perception of Incongruity: A Paradigm," *Journal of Personality*, 1949, 18, 206-223.

[97] A classic philosophical treatment of different approaches to gathering and interpreting information is C. West Churchman's *The Design of Inquiring Systems* (New York: Basic Books, 1971).

[98] Paul J. H. Schoemaker, "Scenario Planning: A Tool for Strategic Thinking," *Sloan Management Review* (Winter 1995), 25–40. For scenario planning books with practical applications, see P. Schwartz, *Art of the Long View* (New York: Doubleday, 1991); Kees van der Heijden, *Scenarios: The Art of Strategic Conversation* (New York: John Wiley, 1996); Gill Ringland, *Scenario Planning* (New York: John Wiley, 1998); Liam Fahey and Robert Randall, eds., *Learning from the Future* (New York: John Wiley, 1998); Paul J. H. Schoemaker, *Profiting from Uncertainty* (New York: Free Press, 2001).

[99] For details, see P. J. H. Schoemaker and G. S. Day, "How to Make Sense of Weak Signals," *MIT Sloan Management Review* 50, no. 3 (Spring 2009): 81–89.

[100] This accidental discovery was told to me by Dr. Hans Vemer, when he was President of Organon International, which was part of Akzo-Nobel. Since then Organon has been sold to Schering Plough. The pharmaceutical industry is replete was such accidental discoveries, from penicillin to Viagra, as chronicled in Morton A. Meyers, *Happy Accidents* (New York: Arcade Publishing, Inc., 2007).

[101] See *http://www.brainyquote.com/quotes/quotes/v/vincent-van389704.html*.

[102] See *http://news.stanford.edu/news/2005/june15/jobs-061505.html*.

[103] Alexander Pope, "An Essay on Criticism."

[104] See *http://forums.randi.org/showthread.php?t=111147*.

[105] For other business examples of learning from mistakes see John C. Maxwell, *Failing Forward: Turning Mistakes into Stepping Stones for Success* (New York: Thomas Nelson, 2007).

[106] Quoted from an interview in the April 2011 *Harvard Business Review*. The entire issue was devoted to exploring the role of failure in business and provides powerful examples of smart CEOs recognizing that you can learn more from failure than success.

[107] See "Top Pros Who Never Had a Lesson," *http://online.wsj.com/article/SB10001424052748703730804576321120772595378.html*.

[108] W. Chan Kim and Renee Mauborgne, *Blue Ocean Strategy: How to Create Uncontested Market Space and Make the Competition Irrelevant* (Cambridge, MA: Harvard Business School Press, 2005).

[109] Sharon Begley, "In Physics, Big Errors Can Get the Ball Rolling toward Big Discoveries," *Wall Street Journal*, September 3, 2004.

[110] See *http://www.cbsnews.com/stories/2010/12/29/60minutes/main7195058_page5.shtml*.

[111] See *http://www.jazzwest.com/articles/improv_1.html*.

[112] *The Speaker's Electronic Reference Collection*, AApex Software, 1994.

[113] James Joyce, *Ulysses* (New York: Vintage, 1990).

[114] Obituary of Fritz Bach, *New York Times*, August 18, 2011.

[115] Story reported by David Tanner in his book *Total Creativity in Business and Industry* (Des Moines, IA: Advanced Practical Thinking, 1997) and recounted by Charles W. Prather, "Use Mistakes to Foster Innovation," *Research Technology Management*, 51, no. 2 (2008).

[116] For specifics, see Howard Raiffa's *Decision Analysis: Introductory Lectures on Choices Under Uncertainty* (Reading, MA: Addison-Wesley, 1968), Paul Kleindorfer, Howard Kunreuther, and Paul J. H. Schoemaker, *Decision Sciences: An Integrative Perspective* (Cambridge: Cambridge University Press, 1993), Ralph Keeney, *Value-Focused Thinking* (Cambridge, MA: Harvard University Press, 1992).

[117] Harry M. Markowitz, *Portfolio Selection: Efficient Diversification of Investments* (New York: John Wiley & Sons, 1959), *http://cowles.econ.yale.edu/P/cm/m16/index.htm.*

[118] Specifically, the Nobel Prize was awarded to Harry Markowitz for having developed the theory of portfolio choice; William Sharpe, for his contributions to the theory of price formation for financial assets, the so-called *Capital Asset Pricing Model* (CAPM); and Merton Miller, for his fundamental contributions to the theory of corporate finance.

[119] The assumptions underlying the capital asset pricing model have since been challenged on both conceptual and empirical grounds. Consequently finance models have been expanded and modified; see Gregory Connor, Lisa Goldberg, and Robert Korajczyk, *Portfolio Risk Analysis* (Princeton, NJ: Princeton University Press, 2010).

Index

About the Author

Paul J.H. Schoemaker is a pioneer in the field of decision sciences, among the first to combine the core ideas of decision theory, behavioral economics, scenario planning, decision theory, and risk management into a set of strategic decision-making tools for managers. He is coauthor of a landmark book on the subject, *Winning Decisions: Getting It Right the First Time* with J. Edward Russo (Doubleday, 2002). Paul is also the founder and executive chairman of Decision Strategies International, Inc. (*www.decisionstrat.com*). Paul is a dedicated educator as well: he is research director of the Mack Center for Technological Innovation at the Wharton School of the University of Pennsylvania, was a professor at the University of Chicago for 12 years, and has given over 100 lectures and executive seminars around the world.

Paul coauthored several books, including *Profiting from Uncertainty* (Free Press, 2002), *Peripheral Vision* with George Day (Harvard Business Review Group, 2006), and *Chips, Clones and Living Beyond 100* with Joyce Schoemaker (Pearson Ltd, 2009). He has written over 100 academic and applied papers, which have appeared in such diverse journals as the *Harvard Business Review*, the *Journal of Mathematical Psychology, Management Science, Journal of Risk and Uncertainty, Behavioral and Brain Sciences*, and the *Journal of Economic Literature*. His writings appear in at least 14 languages. His scholarly articles rank in the top one percent of academic citations globally as measured by the International Science Index (*www.ISIHighlyCited.com*). Ten years after its appearance, his 1995 article, "Scenario Planning," ranked second as the most reprinted publication in the 50-year history of the *MIT Sloan Management Review*.

Paul also serves as the chairman of two family-owned businesses: one is a wholesale distribution company based in Ohio that sells safety salt, water softener, mulch, and related products (*www.publicsalt.com*). The other company is a specialized food-additives business based in the Netherlands that offers customized mixes and ingredients for the meat, fish, and dairy industry in and beyond Europe (*www.vaessen-schoemaker.nl*). In addition, Paul served as a board member of the Decision Education Foundation (*www.decision-education.org*), and continues to support this philanthropic organization, which teaches decision-making skills to adolescents, in partnership with many U.S. high schools across the country. A native of the Netherlands, Paul lives on the East Coast with his wife, Joyce; they have two children.

About Wharton Digital Press

Wharton Digital Press was established to inspire bold, insightful thinking within the global business community. In the tradition of The Wharton School of the University of Pennsylvania and its online business journal *Knowledge @Wharton*, Wharton Digital Press uses innovative digital technologies to help managers meet the challenges of today and tomorrow.

As an entrepreneurial publisher, Wharton Digital Press delivers relevant, accessible, conceptually sound, and empirically based business knowledge to readers wherever and whenever they need it. Its format ranges from ebooks and enhanced ebooks to mobile apps and print books available through print-on-demand technology. Directed to a general business audience, the Press's areas of interest include management and strategy, innovation and entrepreneurship, finance and investment, leadership, marketing, operations, human resources, social responsibility, business-government relations, and more.

http://wdp.wharton.upenn.edu

UNIVERSITY *of* PENNSYLVANIA
Aresty Institute of Executive Education

About The Wharton School

The Wharton School of the University of Pennsylvania—
founded in 1881 as the first collegiate business school—is
recognized globally for intellectual leadership and ongoing
innovation across every major discipline of business education.
The most comprehensive source of business knowledge in
the world, Wharton bridges research and practice through
its broad engagement with the global business community.
The School has more than 4,800 undergraduate, MBA,
executive MBA, and doctoral students; more than 9,000
annual participants in executive education programs; and an
alumni network of 86,000 graduates.

http://www.wharton.upenn.edu